Reimagined:
Bridging this World and Others

NIMROD INTERNATIONAL JOURNAL

Reimagined:
Bridging this World and Others

Nimrod International Journal is indexed in
Humanities International Complete

ISBN: 978-0-9860178-3-4   ISSN: 0029-053X
Volume 57, Number 2
Spring/Summer 2014

THE UNIVERSITY OF TULSA — TULSA, OKLAHOMA

This isseue is dedicated to

Joe Dempsey,
1925–2014,
fast friend of Nimrod
and enemy of all that is false,
including pretentious writing,

and to

Nancy Feldman,
1922–2014,
supporter of all the arts and education,
who loved poetry when read aloud to her;
knew a fine story and told one,
and always embraced her family,
which grew larger each moment.

Acknowledgements

This issue of *Nimrod* is funded by donations, subscriptions, and sales. *Nimrod* and The University of Tulsa acknowledge with gratitude the many individuals and organizations that support *Nimrod*'s publication, annual prize, and outreach programs: *Nimrod*'s Advisory and Editorial Boards; and *Nimrod*'s Angels, Benefactors, Donors, and Patrons.

ANGEL ($1,000+)
Ellen and Steve Adelson, Joan Flint (deceased), Susan and Robert Mase, The Ruth K. Nelson Trust, Aldean Newcomb and George Krumme, Lisa Ransom and David Flesher, Susan Flint Seay, Ann Daniel Stone, Mary Lee Townsend and Burt Holmes, Randi and Fred Wightman, The John Steele Zink Foundation

BENEFACTOR ($500+)
Ivy and Joseph (deceased) Dempsey, Kimberly and Brad Doenges, Marion and William Elson, Nancy (deceased) and Raymond Feldman, Stephani Franklin, Bruce Kline, Sandra and Dobie Langenkamp, Francine Ringold, Jane Wiseman

DONOR ($100+)
Teresa and Alex Adwan, Helen Arnold, Margaret and Charles Audrain, Diane Burton, Mary Coates, Katherine and John Coyle, TD Design, Patricia Eaton, Linda Feagin, Ken Fergeson, Sherri and Stuart Goodall, E. Ann Graves, Mrs. James Hardwick, Ellen Hartman, Nancy and William Hermann, Linda Jennings, Carol Johnson, Elizabeth and Sam Joyner, The Kerr Foundation, Therese Young Kim, Marjorie and David Kroll, Robert LaFortune, Roberta Marder, Carol McGraw, Connie Murray, James McGill, Geraldine McLoud, Catherine Gammie Nielsen, Lynne and John Novack, Donna O'Rourke and Tom Twomey, Pamela Pearce, Judy and Roger Randle, Andrea Schlanger, Joan and Harry Seay, Diane and James Seebass, Fran and Bruce Tibbetts, Sharon Walsh, Peter Walter, Melissa and Mark Weiss, The Kathleen Patton Westby Foundation, Marlene Wetzel, Penny Williams, Josephine Winter

PATRON ($50+)
Marian Bovaird, Connie Cronley, Linda and William Epperson, Joann and Robert Franzen, Diane Glancy, Leslie and Chris Matthies, Katie and Ron Petrikin, Peggy Rew, Julie Skye, Linda and Bruce Stoesser, Renata and Sven Treitel, Judith Ungerman, Krista and John Waldron, Ann Watson, Ruth and Kenneth Weston, Linda Woolford, Maria and Yevgeny Yevtushenko

TABLE OF CONTENTS

Editor's Note: Reimagined

When I was child, one of my favorite books for my mother to read to me at bedtime was a collection called *Fifty Famous Fairy Tales*, containing un-Disneyfied versions of classic fairy tales. While I listened to these stories hundreds of times, it never occurred to me that there might be other ways of telling them. I was thirteen when I discovered the novel *Beauty* by Robin McKinley, a young adult retelling of "Beauty and the Beast" in which Beauty reads, rides horses, and has agency far beyond the girl in the fairy tale that I knew. Reading *Beauty* was a kind of magic for me, an awakening to the idea that stories, even famous ones, could be fluid, that they could contain unexplored corners, that they could be changed to provide new meaning and experience. As an adult reader and writer, I return to this idea often.

At heart, we are writers because stories have meant something to us. They have shaped the way that we view the world and ourselves. We return to our favorite stories over and over again, rereading and remembering them throughout many phases of our lives. As we remember them, we are already reimagining them—changing them, making them our own. And sometimes we go a step further by taking stories that we love and intentionally remaking them into something new.

Reimagined: Bridging this World and Others contains poetry, fiction, and creative nonfiction that reimagines fairy tales, myths, historical events, and family legends, as well as work that reimagines voice, poetic form, art, and even language via translation. From Liz Kay, Michael Boccardo, and Tayler Klein come spooky and provocative retellings of Hansel and Gretel, Rapunzel, and Snow White. Celisa Steele, Amy Vaniotis, and Nancy Takacs explore new sides of Eve, Penelope, and Echo, while Gail Peck, Carolyn Kreiter-Foronda, and Scott Elder give us ekphrastic poems that make us think again about familiar paintings. Leo Haber and Myrna Stone take on the voices of J. Robert Oppenheimer and Martin Luther. Nadia Ibrashi twists the pantoum a little, and Denise Duhamel and Julie Marie Wade play with our expectations of a collaborative essay.

In short, this new issue of *Nimrod* lets us enjoy the stories that we love best in intriguing, fresh, thought-provoking, and sometimes disturbing reimaginings. It offers us a bridge from what we expect to what we have not yet imagined, from this world into myriad others.

Eleanor Leonne Bennett, photograph

Sequel

Dear Husband and King,
I'm writing to you because I'm afraid
someone is rewriting our story.

Lately, your mother has been
licking her lips and eyeing
the kids rather strangely,
and knowing her ogreish
lineage, I fear she admires
Daisy's round arms and Dawn's
dimpled knees with
other than grandmotherly affection.

I know how important your war must be,
but I'm worn out trying to make
my lamb *printanier* and *blanquette de veau*
tender enough to please her. Unless
you return to the castle with haste,
we're in imminent danger of losing,
my dear, our happily ever after.

The Book of Life

His Father had a Book he wrote in,
    Jesus said, who must have thought
we believed in books that much.
    My father remembered that every day
one summer in high school he recorded,
    "Went to band practice. Wind blew."

Young, I reported the temperatures
    myself, and occasional thoughts
for a month, the time I liked Nancy
    more than Marilyn after all.

My grandfather entered me
    into life the way an angel might
not knowing my name: "December 7th:
    a son born to Wendell and Johnnie."
December 8th, he noted omnisciently,
    "3 inches snow — streets very slick."

Does it matter whether Jesus was wrong?
    Unto us is born a book. We
keep trying to write in it, we keep
    trying to read in it. We keep trying
to think of a better title.

Rewriting Beyrouth

You read like the error
of a child who's just learnt
the magic, the possibility,
of combining letters.

To write you down
is like writing with rain, with thirst.
To spell you is always
a spell gone wrong,

a potion where one forgets,
or invents,
a thread of light, footsteps,
the scent of coffee.

Beyroot for the mud, the search,
the reaching out,
but also for the certainty
of the earth.

Byerouth for
the Arabic effect,
the right pronunciation,
for the sound of distance
in the cold. *Byerouth*
for a transliteration on the walls
of a café *à la mode*.

Beyroute for streets
flickering backwards
like memories into my head.

I prefer to keep
the *th* at the end,
absolute like a *the*,
hesitant like a lisp,
a small *h* masquerading as silence,
a journey interrupted or not knowing
how to end.

Pantoum of the Turkish coffee

The first time I drank Turkish coffee,
I sat in a castle by the Nile.
A blue fountain misted the room, moist
heat, as I mourned my uncle's death.

I sat in a castle by the Nile,
thick coffee grounds stunning my mouth, a sudden
heat, as I mourned my uncle's death,
trying not to spit, gulping the ungulpable.

Thick coffee grounds stunned my mouth,
I wondered why people drank this stuff,
trying not to spit, gulping the ungulpable,
heavy silt like muddied banks of the Nile.

I wondered why people drank this stuff,
perhaps for the way coffee settles at the bottom
—heavy silt like muddied banks of the Nile—
and how one's fortune shows through the cracks.

Perhaps for the way coffee settles at the bottom,
weird crossed streaks, scribbled names of saints,
and how one's fortune shows through the cracks,
mysterious harbingers of fate.

Weird crossed streaks, scribbled names of saints;
Bless the coffee-drinker, the seer-reader says,
and how one's fortune shows through the cracks,
beware the webbed finger of fate.

Bless the coffee-drinker, the seer-reader says,
but I'm easily spooked and don't want to
beware the webbed finger of fate.
I'd rather be surprised, not anticipate a new disaster.

I'm easily spooked and don't want to
have my coffee grounds read;
I'd rather be surprised, not anticipate a new disaster—
remember the first time I drank Turkish coffee.

Let Us Praise Brown

for it eases us into the stark season,
for it is the color of earth-
worms, the color of dung
and of dirt which generates
the green we celebrate
and the popple's silvery
leaves shivering in the wind,
and without which nothing
can live.

Let us praise brown
for it is the color of homespun
poverty which joyful Francis wore,
for it is the raiment of eagles,
of summer rabbits and of the wren
which makes a joyous noise at Matins,
and let us praise brown for it is the color
of acorns, raining from oak trees
sharp against roof and road,
sustaining the bear's long sleep,
and of pine cones lying
in wait for fire to melt their hearts
into green.

Let us praise brown
for it is the color and richly
pleasing smell of coffee
beans roasting which belies
their bitter black brew,
and let us praise the tasteful
brown shade begotten of cream
for otherwise we would taste
in every mugful and many times daily
our lives. So also let us praise brown
for it is the color of the bitter cacao bean
which belies its brown sweetness sung
in many tongues: chocolate, *choclad*,

suklaa, sjokolade, kokoleka,
for it is bliss, for without it love
might die.

Let us praise brown
for its mute simplicity,
for its unobtrusiveness,
for its meekness and humility,
and for the self-effacing way it dims
neon lights, street lights, house lights, billboard lights,
until the city beds down in brown-out and the stars
revive.

Shoshana Kertesz, photograph

After the Wedding

But it was as beautiful as most things as
the napkins on the sand were trivial
as bowed narcissus or as a gull has
to circle earth nine times—the sheet-metal

sea beneath its gray wings—before it dies
to become another spool of feather
and flesh on the shore where you, still too shy
to outlast the party, stood by the weathered

car: the sunflowers on the windshield dried,
the roses on the beach gathering dew:
the dozen you held. The heat clenched their red
heads shut. You said language was a blue

Japanese vase cemented together,
cracked lip, no husk or center for flowers.

If We Say Blue

> *. . . in truth, only spoken words can be heard.*
> —Earl Shorris, "The Last Word"*

If we say blue, the word that begins with the voiced, bi-labial plosive stop
and then blends into the liquid el before gliding through an eerie diphthong
(or does it just hang out along the back in one long continuo?)
before it ends with our lips pursed
almost for a kiss,

do we hear a saxophone under the tracks through the thunder of trains,
and is it like sparks that seem to lick the hot steel
sending a mind-splitting screech, or is it a scream, perhaps our own,
all the way through the heartland, all along the river, all the way down
to our delta?

And do we feel the hot breath on our neck blown by a lover
before she blows the candle out, sweet with wine through lips
gorged with kissing, willing and wet (how like we this?),
or do we put out the light and then put out the light knowing
the other kiss?

And do we see ultramarine that cost Renaissance patrons four florins
an ounce, or the blue of a Yucatan butterfly, the hue and intensity
beyond our naming, beyond even *azul, azul marino*, and *cobalto*
that reduce the nine ancient words, leaving six butterflies
visible only by the Maya,

Or perhaps it is one of the lost blue butterflies only the Maya know
working its way back through the earth and air, pushing and shaping
our vocal chords and tongue, teeth and lips to make something
whole again, to bring something back,
the sorrow of something lost.

---

*"There are nine different words in Maya for the color blue . . .but just three Spanish
translations, leaving six butterflies that can be seen only by the Maya, proving beyond
doubt that when a language dies six butterflies disappear from the consciousness of the
earth," *Harpers*, August 2000.

Psalm of Waiting

1

For days I walk through silence,
the dogs following at my heels,
room to room, upstairs to the loft.

Sometimes I lie on the floor
and play with them, tossing
the stuffed hedgehog down the staircase.

When I sit quietly rocking
they lie down beside the chair.
They comfort me.

They follow me
to the garden and watch
while I inspect lantana

and crush the dried blossoms
of summer's drought
between my fingers.

2

On the drive to the cabin the dogs
curl on the backseat, content with change.
I stop at Webb's fruit stand, buy Loring peaches

and honey from Sourwood Mountain.
Climbing Hwy 181, I wonder
if this downpour will flood the creek.

How to keep mice from nesting
in the bottom kitchen drawer.
What to do about the giant

hemlock growing too close
to the cabin door. I don't want
to be there when it happens.

3

This is what I'm thinking,
towing my brother's death
up the mountain.

And when I drive through a flash flood,
he appears, standing beside a ditch,
rain pelting his ballcap, hitch-hiking his way back.

He slides onto the passenger seat,
asks if we can stop at the country store,
buy a loaf of white bread.

4

The cabin waits in darkness
for me to unlock the back door,
switch on the lights.

When I fill the water bowls,
grief pours from the faucets.

The dogs lick my hands.

—for Ray, 2010

The Other Universe

A doe watched my brother Pete watch me get out of my car,
carry the groceries.

Then he made a movie of the doe watching us,
of me standing by a lodgepole pine.

We stowed my stuff in his apartment, headed into nearby woods
that were strewn with old tires and broken bags of trash.
An abandoned refrigerator had landed face down.
He wondered aloud if there could be a body inside.

After our walk, we sat in his kitchen, heard,
through thin plasterboard, the woman next door cough.

✼

I died thirteen times in Vietnam, he told me.

Once I got shot by a diamond.
The person's body shuts down as if he's dead,
but the body's working to get the diamond out.

Another time, crossing a river on pilings, I got shot by Vietcong.
The guys I was with had to carry me.

Then we were in a hole, threw mortars into the village.

The others didn't seem to mind killing.
I wondered if it was because they'd been killed themselves
and gone to a parallel universe. Every so often,
I met people like that in Vietnam.

Only some can go back and forth, others can't, and,
for a few, there's a last time. Then they stay there.

Maybe schizophrenia is when
someone carries the memory of both worlds.

The last time, you don't feel anything, you don't know anything,
nothing hurts.

❁

Next door, the woman coughed.
He worried she might have a disease
that could travel through the wall.

We watched the movie of the doe and me and made dinner,
cleared a space on the kitchen table, shared spaghetti, salad, bread.
I put two packages of candles on the cake.

He made a movie of the cake, of us lighting the candles,
me singing Happy Birthday, him blowing out all the flames
in one breath. We watched the movie.
During quiet parts, we could hear the woman cough.

❁

I think the fourteenth death was final.

His face above the blown-out candles.
For a long time, I wondered what he wished.

Kathryn Dunlevie, "Sing," mixed media on album cover

Seven Fishburn, Up

Lots of Vietnam vets were back; we knew some of them. They returned quiet, fidgety, and not yet ready, they said, to get educated. Thanks to the G. I. Bill, they had time. They'd drive fast cars in loud blues and yellows, rear tires jacked up, their eyes shaded with mirrored glasses. They smoked and drank and got jobs as security guards or cops. In Madison, Wisconsin, things went from jumpy to frantic, and one evening Brett called me and my friend Selena to come see Freddie sail his toy boat. Freddie worked the joystick on his remote, the jib and main sails fanned out, both made from red bandanas. Nice stern, nice bow, the vets said. We said, Get lost, and cheered Freddie on. The boat skimmed Mendota's waves: scarlet and bright as our UW t-shirts. It plowed farther and farther, the boat, and not arrow-straight. It dove. It plunged, ours a lovely boat lake, anyone would agree. Freddie handled the remote, steering gracefully, and did not let up. He stood on the grassy knoll where Dr. Carpenter had picnicked that warm April day before he joined the Marines. Gorgeous blessing. Dr. C had stood on that grassy rise, ice chest nearby, and invited all of us to enjoy a sandwich and a beer. We accepted his offer and circled around to begin the feast.

Fine, fine, he said to us. Gather in. Ham and cheese, a Bud? Selena loved beer, and me too, beer, ale common as air.

We ate the sandwiches, the Buds perfectly cold. Have another, he said, in memory of Hemingway, he said, close enough for us to whiff his cologne. His eyes were clear, and the amber color of the beer would bring up the blood in his cheeks, too ready to spill.

We had seconds, and on the shore of the lake we took off our shoes to wade in. Most of the girls from Dr. C's class were there and the artsy one, Theresa. She took a misstep. She was up to her neck and we swam to her. Dr. C knelt beside her, reminding me of a priest at last rites. He gazed up at us, winking, and said, "I commend Theresa's soul into God's hands," and we felt that was fitting since death eliminated her from the competition. Him we wished to save us.

We picnicked until evening light turned soft then; listening to the insect chorus sing in the approaching night, we said adieu.

Now Selena and I watched the boat sail where Dr. Carpenter had knelt, and on the pier beside Freddie was another boat, which he switched to, a sturdier, longer craft that could venture the great distance near Mendota's middle, in a curvy line then a circle, a figure eight, the infinity sign, and Selena said, "I have a feeling. Something's come over me — Dr. C's on the mend, coming full-circle. He's not going to pull a gun-in-the-mouth Hemingway." Nice try, I said, though she'd gotten me wishing against all odds: Freddie, only a vet we barely knew, arrived out of the blue to sail a boat; we two friends, still sane, who were called to watch.

❊ ❊ ❊

Dr. Carpenter is sick. Mother is sick. Aubrey learns electricity at community college in all-male classes, an electrical genius at eighteen, so writes Aunt Daisy, whom I picture, her hair set in concrete curls, lips puckered with the purse-strings of age.

Aunt Daisy wants to remain in touch, Cincinnati like Madison only hillier, she writes, all seven bluffs alive with dogwoods and magnolias, irises not far behind and Easter soon, after Palm Sunday, after Passion Week, fish and fries, Friday food. Remember your religion, she writes. Don't ever lose your *faith* (a word I think should weigh more on the page, weighed down and leaden). We have an epidemic of the sick, your mother one of the fallen — pneumonia — but healing up. She sends a photo to show me, though Mom looks thin and grim as always, her pet canary in a birdcage behind her. In the letter she has put another picture, of the boyfriend, Dow, a strange name, Aubrey's steady with talk of marriage. Ay yi yi! she writes.

In Madison, a spring snow has arrived, I write Aunt Daisy, our winter togs already traded for lighter wear, one sweater layered over another and one more — but life is good, good. The roomies remaining, Brett and me and Henry, Jesus, Henry, but Michael, Nick, Richard, and Frank have gone back home, talk of the draft ending soon, the war not far behind, though the suicide rate among returnees is on the rise if you're stressed enough. No surprise if Aunt Daisy declared that was why Dad succumbed.

Oh, really?

Make room for Selena, says Selena, who, as she moves into Nick's room, wonders aloud why women were not drafted.

Selena answers herself with the Fifth Commandment, Thou shalt not kill, then amends it: Unless it's wartime and you're a man. And it's always wartime. After Dr. Carpenter is deployed, I write to

Aunt Daisy, and again after Dr. C returns off his rocker. He was a professor, I write, then Vietnam occupiers messed things up for him.

✻ ✻ ✻

Freddie brings his vet friends to our house, popping beers and grilling dogs, burgers. Some have one good ear and some limp. Some hold all the stress in and some are fakers, Selena says. Are we running a motel? Brett asks, but he pitches in every chance. None of us wants them to stay overnight, for weeks and more. We wait at grocery store back doors asking for day-olds, bread, soft tomatoes, slimy greens. Sometimes restaurants give us leftovers from the day. We're risking food poisoning. We help where we can. Brett volunteers at the Red Cross and brings home cots and blankets, and Selena waits tables, earning enough for fresh fruit and vegetables, dates the bartender.

We offer what we can.

The vets have tales to tell and Selena and I are not so keen to hear the stories of ear trophies, razed villages, Hotel Hanoi, the hot, hot jungles. They gave up on quiet and cool comfort. "Rotting messily in their graves — " one begins, his unfinished sentence fluttering like a kite tail. We unfold the cots. They stay awhile, duffle bags for pillows. They drink beer and grill grub and trade tales. Rumor mill has it there's hospitality here, they say, and good-lookers with generous ears. Word on the street says this is a place to rest, not to worry about being refused. The living and dining rooms, the furniture pushed to the walls, leave a wide area for stretching, for composing, coming back to yourself. We're glad to help, we tell them. We'll share our house, but we're not medics, just UW students working our way through. Mostly, they want to tell stories: of shrapnel, of gunshot wounds, amputations; of drugs, sex, death; of the prayer to Saint Raphael for a safe trip that protected him there and back, his talisman, a prayer he had tattooed on his chest, his heart, to express gratitude for a prayer so strong he returned unscathed, if you don't count the things he saw and did and heard.

"Gah!" a vet says. "For protection you recite, 'Yea, though I walk through the valley of the shadow of death, I will fear no evil, for I am the evilest son of a bitch in the valley.'"

Some make their way from the bus depot carrying a bad smell. We give them soap, a towel, point out the shower, and they say they "hounded it here" from the VA Hospital or from the church or from family. They assure us they'll be on their way as soon as the street noises stop detonating bombs under their pillows or the radio quits signaling them orders to take out the village or the potted ferns withdraw their leafy canopies that grow thick and viney in all directions, entombing them in their overgrowth. "Agent Orange," some call out in their sleep.

Some of the vets are good-looking under the grime. One by the name Andrew says he'd been a point man. "That's bait," he says. "I'd initiate an ambush then keep firing when the bloodbath commenced. There's nothing so sweet as the smell of death in the morning," he says, trapping a tear under his fingernail. But he switches that, saying he was a photographer for the military and, later, that he was a medic. He yawns on his cot and asks us to play some music to help him get to sleep. Next day he is AWOL, a kitchen's worth of supplies gone with him.

"Look who lied through his teeth," Brett says. "And me without my rifle." But Selena and I had been taken in.

Then Brett plays the guitar for the handsome Ray. "This will soothe you," he says, and it works; the pair of them, Selena and Ray, hot pepper running in their veins, depart, same as the food in the pantry. She'll live to regret the day she laid eyes on him, Brett says. I am caught between love and free love, Brett says.

We listen to their Zippo poems as they recite them; the vets tell us writing calms their nerves. They write of POWs, Charlie, muddy foxholes, belief and disillusionment, loss and commitment, sad, angry, funny rhymes and lines. It would heal any heart to express long-held images, Brett says, ignoring the violent rage in many.

A Cincinnatian named Seth comes by for coffee, waving me over from the front porch where I'm watering pansies. It's a nippy day. He's from the hospital, he tells me, and is on his way to Chicago to see a nurse he met in recovery who'd given him her address when he was bandaged head to toe and doesn't know what he looks like. I offer him milk and sugar and ask him how he knows she'll like to see him. His face looks stricken as if the thought is a bad smell. He says, "Me? You blind?" and I shake my head every time I recall his hubris.

Selena's family discovers that she's run off with a stranger and puts her on notice. Brett and I take her out for a farewell dinner, me watching from the front porch as her VW beater moves toward the lake, toward the grassy picnic knoll. Years have passed since we walked into Dr. C's classroom together, and she is kindness and generosity, a friend, better than any. As a parting gift I give her the etched crystal wine decanter Mom sent for my last birthday, the dainty glass protected with layers of tissue paper as my mother has sent it. I want you to have it, I say. It's just right for you.

The vets have a way of helping us know what's precious.

"So pretty," Selena says, opening the box. "I'll put it to good use."

"With Ray?" I say.

"Ma-ay-bee," she says.

She lifts out the decanter.

"It was his?"

"Whose?"

"Your father's?"

"Mother's," I say. "Mother's and father's. A wedding gift."

"Whiff of Chardonnay," she says, returning the cap.

An ache in the region of my heart.

We listen to the vets in the living and dining rooms, not so many as before, Brett has decided, since Selena's leaving, and I, too, will be gone before long, having applied to grad school and gotten in. As expected, Brett says, since I'm a born teacher and why not go all the way to a Ph.D. before standing behind a lectern in front of my first class.

"If I had a farm in Vietnam and a home in hell, I'd sell my farm and go home," the vets recite from downstairs, wishing Selena and I were there to laugh and ahh while kneading bread and stirring the pot, our eyes bright. "When I die, bury me face down so the whole world can kiss my ass." "I love the fucking army and the army loves fucking me."

*   *   *

If he were older, he might be wearing fatigues, be hard of hearing, walk with a cane, if he'd been drafted, so likely he's younger than he appears.

"Joshua Moore," he says.

"Lydia Bridgewell," I say, conscious of my hair corralled in a terrible ponytail.

He offers to share his bottle of wine and I accept. I am at the bus station way ahead of boarding, travelling below the Mason- Dix-

on Line, Selena said. Call and tell me about Southern hospitality.
I've always heard about Southern hospitality.

"Here's spit in your eye," says Joshua Moore.

He has a long face, square, and sports a necktie thinner than
his mustache, cigarettes in a breast pocket.

"Bottoms up," I say. "To Archangel Raphael," I say, because
Selena would be pleased—prayers to this saint, she has come to
discover, since the vet's miraculous story, can also find a good spouse
and lead to happy meetings—a dressy prayer, that, the good china
of prayers. Besides, now that I'm twenty-one, I can say and do as
I please, Southern hospitality null and void in the Midwest, I would
tell Selena. Though not for long, as shortly I have found a seat and
watch out the window as Madison unspools behind me.

I ride through the night by highway to Nashville—this Greyhound packed to the gills with returned vets. I see them jerk in
their sleep and come to with a jolt from nightmares that must be
doozies, and I see their strained faces reflected in the black windows.
Strange, I write Selena, departing chilly Wisconsin for warm, even
hot, climes. And the jolt might be a stab instead, it might be a jab.
The strained faces might be saying, "Don't. Stop."

The bus driver loves President Nixon. Many call him Tricky
Dick—well deserved, too, Joshua Moore states, remember the My
Lai Massacre? Remember how he handled the Kent State killings?
"God grant me the serenity," I begin inside my head, ". . . and the
weapons to know the difference."

He sits beside me without my asking him to, a magazine open
on his lap, the word *bluegrass* visible at a glance. I put aside my letter
to Selena and smooth down the cover to see what kind of magazine
interests him. The bus is cool, as I wrap a throw (Brett's from his
grandmother, one he's never had a use for) around my shoulders. I
finger my gold hoop earrings, my lucky charms, well, the diamond
slivers in each one, the pair a gift from Aubrey to her maid of honor,
me, on her wedding day. I check the clasps to ensure they do not
come loose during the trip on this long, dark road.

Yes, I say to Joshua Moore, I know about Nixon.

"That he beat Humphrey's a travesty. Tragic!"

"Terrible," I say.

"Catastrophic!" he nearly shouts into the night. I wonder if he
is loud for the benefit of pro-war passengers, a unit returning from
Vietnam where they have, for God and country, tried to bomb the
communists back into the Stone Age.

"Of course," I say, and Joshua Moore chucks me under the chin and returns to his magazine. I find my letter to Selena, writing to her of bluegrass and conscientious objectors and Canada.

The sandwich Joshua Moore shares is more than welcome. In my rush to pack and reach the station, I forgot about food—closer to the truth, I do not have the money to spare above the taxi fare from Nashville's depot to Belmont's admissions office. If there had been a cheaper way to cross the Mason-Dixon Line, I'd have chosen it.

"I'm too adamant for you," Joshua Moore says. He stares at the highway and from this angle I find his profile attractive, his angular jaw and chin. He might be twenty-one or younger. He drums his fingers on one knee. It seems he is a musician even without an instrument in hand.

"Not at all. I'm writing a letter."

"Family?"

"Pardon?"

"Friend? A fiancé?"

Joshua Moore drums both knees. I swallow. "The war ended it," I lie, or not: perhaps I am telling Joshua about Dr. Carpenter, about the vets' stories, their poems, about Freddie who sailed a boat. Freddie had up and left like so many, the sailboat adrift in the garage loft, the red bandana jib and mainsails lowered, in a cobwebbed corner, forgotten. No one would lower the ladder folded into the garage ceiling, and Brett said the steps were too rickety to hold our weight. "We don't want to be mistaken for war vets, do we?" he said.

By this time, Brett had had it up to here. He wasn't the Pope of Good Will and Free Stuff. Yet, the vets were drawn to that house like squirrels to Hostess Sno Balls; they showed up like misty breath on a cold day. At times they would walk right in the back door pleading for respite from the anti-war sentiment. Selena baked loaf after loaf, lopping off big chunks to wrap in foil with a dollop of butter or jam. "'They wrote in the old days that it is sweet and fitting to die for one's country. But in modern war there is nothing sweet nor fitting in your dying. You will die like a dog for no good reason,'" Selena said, quoting Hemingway from one of Dr. Carpenter's lectures. Brett, Selena, and I were the ones who were dedicated, walking the streets of Madison that were filled with "Get the Hell out of Vietnam." Sometimes, protestors passed by and waved, hippies or students in bellbottoms and tie-dyes—post-Woodstockers. Sometimes vets, fists pumping, chanted, "Don't tell us about Vietnam because we've been there."

✿ ✿ ✿

Joshua Moore snatches my suitcase from under the bus storage. He says the cheering section is for the returning vets, since who turns out to greet a Greyhound? By section he refers to the reporters—men and women with microphones and cameras. The vets give interviews, mug for pictures inside the depot, family members flapping painted signs: "Support Our Boys in Vietnam." "Bomb Hanoi," they read.

The taxi cabs are at the curb and Joshua Moore, taking in the clouds overhead thick as gray wool, asks if we can share one. I say yes. I have some spare cash now, and I am on the south side of the Mason-Dixon Line and I am heading for Belmont University, where I will gather all the information I need, first and foremost about apartments for rent. In fact, I have no idea about how I will live, only my acceptance, and the course requirements, in the inside pocket of my suitcase. I will earn a puny stipend in return for teaching one class each semester.

Now Joshua Moore hands me a note with his address written on it. I take it and step out of the cab, resting one hand on the shut door, getting my bearings; the idea that I have moved south, alone once again, yanks like a wild dog on a leash and howls.

✿ ✿ ✿

Have you met with your advisor? Has he signed off on your classes? Have your professors admitted you?

I open my folder, search for letters. The office I have walked into, fluorescent ceiling lights, says Registrar. I hand over the folder, unable to find the required documents, to the clerk behind the high counter. "I slept on a bus last night," I say brainlessly.

She gestures to a bench behind me then retreats to a cubicle. Beneath her makeup, her skin is wearing through. Her hair is cut short, bangs across the front, stick-out ears, a style for hot weather. I see a gathering of students, shag cuts, fringe, jugears, boys and girls alike in the marbled corridor, near a colorful mosaic. They look like boys, the girls. They wear baggy loose-fitting tees, talking, laughing, their heads thrown back. Are you new here? they ask me.

The clerk's face is not boyish; it is puffy and stern, her gray-streaked hair a size too small for her round head.

"Okay then," she says.

"Good to go," I say.

"Your folder?" she says.

She returns to her cubicle and vanishes inside it once more—only her skimpy hair visible above one wall's horizon. I prop my elbows atop the counter. Spring aromas waft in from somewhere. I am in Nashville, I now realize: the humid green lawns, air thick as lacquer, and the fragrances that follow like an echo, convince me I've been too long in the Midwest. Lilacs, new leaves, mown grass fresh as rain, B.O. I fold my arms on the counter, my head heavy from a night on a bus now at rest on them. Has the woman forgotten about me, my folder?

"What's going on here?" Dad says beside me. His voice is just as I remember it. Why is he here? To stop me?

"My advisor signed off," I say. I'm happy to see him. "You signed off without a good-bye as I recall."

"Yes."

"Then there we were."

"Yes," he says. "May or November, what difference did it make?"

"But Mom," I say, though I try to tone the edge down.

"Yes," he says.

He looks at me sadly, as he had in those last weeks—lost, unbelieving, depressed, a psychiatrist would have diagnosed him, had he seen a psychiatrist, which he should have, I wanted to tell him—not for a cure, of course—for an end with dignity, perhaps. But I don't want to hurt him. His red hair is so pale; is he already fading out? He wears work pants and a collared shirt, sleeves to the wrists. Now he unbuttons one cuff and rolls it back. His arm was not always so scarred. He had been a sturdy strong man.

"I'm sorry," he says.

You were sound asleep, the stern-faced clerk says. Her eyes snag and hold me. She says, I tapped on your arm, and you were talking with someone, not me, then you woke up with a start. Are you all right?

She gestures once more toward the bench. I tilt my head to the wall. She gets me a cup of water. I thank her and close my eyes. Can you spare a sandwich? I want to ask.

I stay on the bench awhile. Not sure how long. Time passes and Joshua Moore is beside me; later he tells me, "Lucky guess you'd run into a snafu at the registrar's."

"Need any help?" he says.

"She'll need this folder," the clerk says, handing Joshua Moore my papers.

"I see," he says. "I see."

※　※　※

I rest my eyes on the way to Joshua Moore's place, an apartment near Broadway, downtown, on Fishburn, up, number seven, spitting distance from Bel's Mont, as he calls it. Joshua Moore extends a hand as I step out of the cab. His fingers are long and thin, his palm wide, a bluegrasser's hand. Mine disappears in his; I find this oddly comforting. It is like the oven mitt at the house in Madison we used for hot dishes from the oven, Selena and I careful not to touch the glove to a red coil and start a fire.

It is evening, streetlights on, reflected on the Cumberland River visible from the back porch. Along the shore neon signs blink and glow, nightlife kicking in soon. Honkytonks, Joshua Moore tells me. Bars and bands, songs and good times.

Joshua Moore carries my backpack to a spare room, no furniture, odds and ends, for storage. He's back a day early, he tells me. His band members will be here tomorrow. He points out the bathroom and gives me clean towels for a shower and a change. "Plenty of clothes in your room"— boxfuls of his old girlfriend's, laundered, folded, he guesses, though he hasn't checked. Neat to a fault.

"You have an ex, too," he says.

He tells me to look around, get comfortable. French doors across one wall open out to the street, brightening up the front room, the light filtering into the kitchen, mingling with the slanted rays from the porch for a cheery effect. It is cozy all in all, which I am trying not to notice. I am trying to keep my balance and listen to Joshua Moore, trying to figure out the sentences that speed my way—about his friend in Wisconsin; he was in Madison to see him before the friend returned to Canada, the friend his ex's brother.

He explains his vehemence on the bus, his loud voice. "They say there's a wild man inside all of us," he says. "If only he'd stay inside." He had been trying to quell his wild man. Later, his words "quell my wild man" I recall as I stand by the French doors, each one curtained in lacy sheers, which, Joshua Moore tells me, were cut from a St. Vincent DePaul wedding dress and stitched and hung by his old girlfriend. The ex's brother, an artist, had chosen the dress and sewn in trim here and there so each panel was unique. Here flowers with pearl centers, here a satin ribbon, did I see? Did I like it?

He has much more to say, Joshua Moore—there's the song he's writing, his instruments, his album collection—but my yawn does not go unnoticed so I say see you later, and I can manage, and in the morning then.

In the extra room, stored items have been pushed to the side and stacked, a mat and sleeping bag on the rug, a sheet and pillow atop. Joshua Moore is cooking; should I get hungry, there's plenty.

I arrange a kind of nest on the floor and turn off the light before settling, and in the dimness I wonder about his ex-girlfriend, her belongings so near—that might be her dulcimer on the shelf, she might have calluses on her fingers from playing, playing. She performed at peace rallies, Joshua Moore said. She helped her brother start his new life in Montreal. That's what she does now, helps those Americans who left for cold and mountains over heat and rice fields. Serving those men is her vocation.

Many are homesick, she would say, they want so badly to return. Boys, barely shaving, she said.

But the ex is no longer in Joshua Moore's life. She's been swept up by a cause, aid to the exiled; most likely she's an outlaw, if helping draft dodgers is illegal. The streetlamp shines in. It is a cupboard of a room, loaded down with cardboard boxes, painted canvases propped on top—a dock in a bay, dark sky, a bright moon the sleepless eye of night, and wavy water all aglitter, all romantic. Orion pulls his bow and other stars, some of them, are near. It must be spring there, too.

I open a box and find her clothes folded and neat, as predicted. They smell—a laundry lemony smell. I will write a letter about this to Selena and about Nashville, worlds apart from Madison, so warm, so restful, the Belmont students, easy and generous: Here's a flowering plant for you. A basket of deep red tomatoes. They talk and sing and dance, their friends in bands, as are their fathers, their grandmothers: The Silver Threads, The Tennessee Family Band, Aunt Selma's Singers. They have always lived here or they have come from Kentucky, Mississippi, the Carolinas. Living at home is common. They study medicine and law, business and English and Kurt Vonnegut's *Slaughterhouse Five*, his World War II experience, the bombing of Dresden. Right now Mr. Vonnegut is working on *Breakfast of Champions*, a scathing satire, something about inequality and changing the world and jokes and doodlings and Dayton, Ohio.

Life is Good! they celebrate. Life is good!

And life is good, everyone gracious and warm, and I am welcome here, I write Selena. I can plant roots and grow here. Of Joshua Moore, I say, we might become more than friends, the Mozart of friends, the bluegrass he plays — Rocky Top, you'll always be home sweet home to me — he's in love with music, and I too am falling head over heels. Bluegrass is his life, he says. Rocky Top, Tennessee, Rocky Top, Tennessee.

I write about my renting Joshua Moore's spare room, and about the stacked boxes now stored in the basement. We are the same age. Besides, Belmont's a mere bicycle ride away, he said, and the rent can't be beat. His logic is bulletproof.

Sixty dollars a month, I said. Gad night a livin'. This is a Southern saying. I pick them up from him and from others in Professor Holley's lit class — Well, I just swaney, I say, or, Catawampus, or, Tie my face to the side of a pig and roll me in mud. And they frown to hear my Midwest twang as if my rounded vowels hurt their ears, offend their sensibilities, before they burst into laughter.

How are you? I write. What's new?

At last a letter from Selena. Her folks have calmed down, she writes. They've helped us put a payment on our house. A fixer-upper. Ray is a handyman, a sweet, quiet man. A regular life, ours. Church on Sundays, bowling on Wednesdays, cleaning and cooking.

A baby! she writes before long. Due next winter. If a boy, we'll call him George, after your dad.

Name

It looks like feathers
scattered on the page
           and sounds like rain
        falling on a tile floor.
    In English
     it clangs like a choo-choo train.

Squeeze the back
    of your tongue on the roof
       of your mouth,
    raise your voice to the pitch
      of a champagne glass
             and sustain that note, letting
        the *sh* of water thicken to metal.

方昌欣
  It means growth and joy,

    but 昌 means also *sing*
      also *long*

                               also *hide*

     and 欣 is *joy*
      but also *star*

                 also *new*
                also *heart*.

My parents call me *Xin Xin*,
    which means gorilla, joy, or star.

My mother's name also has three characters
    she spells out separately,
       Feng   Di   Chen
    each syllable distinct
       as a stone dropped in water.

My father prefers a westernized version
    with a hyphen —

                Neng-yu Fang.

I have had all of these:
at 9 I was   *Fang Chang Xin*
               at 9 ½   *Chang Xin Fang*
                    at 12   *Chang-xin Fang*
                         and at 15   *Changxin,*
     no spaces, hyphens, or capitals,
          continuous as *Angela, Margaret,* or *Mary.*

Sometimes I am tired of my name,
          want instead to be tulip, maple, or cherry tree,

               to need no introduction.
Sometimes I forget my name
          and I call myself *Clarissa.*
               I like the implication of
                              clarity.

My name is three butterflies
          that fly away when I approach them,
     their wings flashing in the sun.

If I keep on thinking
                         it explodes like a star —

          chang xin —   singing joy —

                    green growth —

little star —

     —faith —

fresh awakening —

               —new heart —

Painting in an Enclosed Field at Saint-Paul Hospital

—*After Vincent van Gogh's* Enclosed Field with Peasant

. . . We, who live by bread, are we not ourselves
very much like wheat . . . to be reaped when we are ripe . . .
—Vincent van Gogh, 1889

Like a peasant
   Devout,
I long to haul wheat
   we rise
in the fertile field, enclosed
   and billow
by the asylum's walls I want
   in venerable breezes
to feel the gentle rocking of
   Roots
the gathered stalks
   unfurl, curl
A prism disperses ocher
   into pulsating soil
Lilac rays define
   Sinewy, we grow
olive trees, cypresses,
   like wild thyme, free
sheltered by the rugged Alpilles
   from the North's cold
In this enclosure I strive to recover
   We flower,
amid a wellspring of light
   the florets: aureate,
At the easel, I do for the wheat
   the stems: limber, sleek
what I have done for the reaper
   Sun-drenched, we spit seeds —
I breathe lissome air
   little eyes loosened —

and paint a peasant, hauling a bundle
            onto holy ground
Wary, my attendant follows me
            Our hearts bloom
wherever I go, earthy yellows,
                They ripen into braided gold
silvery grays, blues spattered
                Earth's tongue unfolds,
over my arms, outstretched
            lets go
like ripened grain
                its wind-borne song

Eleanor Leonne Bennett, photograph

Young Girl Standing against a Background of Wheat

after van Gogh, 1890

I had dismissed her,
not drawn by her face
or expression, the paint flat
on the page, and in another book,
this image inverted.
Van Gogh was always in search
of models, unable to pay them.
This one's hands and fingers too long.

It was the dress
that made me look closely —
pink dots, and beside her swirls of poppies.
Her straw hat flops over her head.
I can't imagine standing in the heat
in high collar, long sleeves, returning
to the same place in similar light and weather.

What did she think of?
Lord, the gnats. She is thin
yet one day her body will thicken,
and children will tug at the hem of her skirt,
and she will never be so still again.
Her hands constantly busy
rocking the cradle, distracted.
No longer this silence, lost in thought,
eyes that give away nothing.

Fairy Tale

He closes his eyes and waits.
He's not supposed to think about how dark.
The backs of his eyes, where vision meets light,
can't picture their last photon.
They make one up. Then two: theories of light,
particles that reconcile the wave.
Pretty soon a sparkler sizzles. You could smell it,
like the warm-up to a seizure. One of those lit sticks
that happy kids attack each other with
on midsummer nights that never ever get dark.
Later on they lick their burns with popsicles.

She reaches the tip of his nose. Barely a peck
that breaks the silence: just a bubble on the surface.
Then one eye then the other with her breath,
a puff that leaves him 20:20. The ocean in his ears
never felt so porous. The first kiss is the high tide
and fresh breeze his hull had learned to dream of.
Afloat, they set sail. The rest is GPS with autopilot.

However, versions vary. Neither once nor once upon
they'd meet at the head of the trail near the tree line.
They had gravity in common. And binoculars —
the kind that gather light. That desert used to be an ocean.
That kiss? A prince would be a frog for one of those.
That wish? It calls for a time-out, a pause
before the happy ever after.

How the Rat Didn't Lose its Tail

When a cat steps inside with a live rat dangling
almost by the tail then drops it on the kitchen tile
and chases it around the house for a few laps,
is that all part of God's plan to teach humans
to think like a rat but faster, to teach rats to pray
while scurrying? What's worse than a dead chipmunk
in the cat's jaws? What's worse than a live chipmunk
in the cat's jaws? How limp is a half-dead chipmunk?
Does a chipmunk play possum? How lively is a live rat
on the run from the law? Questions like these
would not be possible without coffee in the morning.

When a cat walks around the wood stove then stops to listen
to something that sounds like its runway's too short,
what does that noise say about chimneys versus nests,
gravity versus lift, getting out of bed in the morning
versus sailing off in the dream that features a boat
floating on air, sails filled with night? Even in the dream
the mind wants to say *starboard* or *port,* to worry over
a lee shore. Even in the heat of the moment the mind skips ahead
from rat in a hall to a maze. When both cats crouch to listen,
when the dogs come to help listen, when the released bird
flies to and out the one open window, when the rat takes the hint
and leaves through the one open door, who would deny their miracle?

And so there are saints, a chorus of saints.
The saint of whole coffee beans ground fresh every morning.
The saint of poems arriving in e-mail. The saint of stories told
and retold from father to son and from son to so on, of tall tales
and mouse tails, of what goes around that comes around
and the funny thing that happened, of orbits that wander
but never decay, of verbs like *decay* applied to orbits,
of clichés that makes us human. Hope springs, faith leaps,
love soars, pride trips and falls then acts like no one noticed.
If we can't be happy ever after, we can at least pretend.

Fossil Resin

Because insects were trapped in amber
we know about the life of arthropods.
Because it's easy to make nothing out of something.
Because my niece Sarah says symbolism is foolish,
she wants to believe what she reads,
what she sees. Because it's too soon to begin
watching the autumn turn into a Maine winter,
leaves dropping like dead things
onto her feet as she shuffles to school. Because it's hard
for me to remember what sixteen feels like, how the future looks
like there's more of everything there. I watch
through the window as if through amber, as men suck leaves off the lawn
into a long white tube, and hope composting happens
somewhere. Because to me, leaves look fine on the grass,
still green in late October. On a new CD
I listen to a story about the life of Jewish men
in a Hungarian work-camp in 1942, how after ten-hour days
of splitting rocks and pushing wheelbarrows uphill they
stood for three hours at attention on a parade ground,
denied light after dark, denied mail, pencil and paper,
news of wives and children. Because it's called "The Invisible Bridge,"
the bridge from that world to this, although I know
we are the same, the people who deliver mail, clean my teeth,
pass my milk and fruit through checkout, teach
my classes. Because so much is trapped in amber,
and adrift on another continent, though amber
is biodegradable as plastic milk jug.

Switching Hands

The sky is disappointed it is not the sea, the tree
that it is not a telephone pole in the city.
My aunt, a physician, longed to deliver mail on foot.
I would be Scylla, or Charybdis, a threat and a charm.
Despite the risks, the carpet picks up its tacks and luffs
towards a known shore. Gulls swoop into telephone books,
almanacs fall into the sea. The sea is a longing. Late,
the Hellenes sculpted an old woman with a market basket
and an old man, a drunk, bare wires of sinews in his neck.
I want to get in the moment of pebbles, secrets, antonyms,
ice cream, insect bites, a teapot, a walk through Trafalgar Square.
But even an apple can be a disappointment, to say nothing
of condiments. Who, a Litvak in Youngstown, does not wish
herself in St. Paul, or Fort Wayne? The lines are long,
the shelves are overflowing, there is too much memory,
too much remembered. It takes longer and longer
to get to the toilet now, climbing over cairns and other memorabilia.
If I met Tomaž Šalamun I would feel differently, but as it is
all he has done is help me perfect the "zsh" sound.
Having grandparents from what once was Russia,
also Poland and Lithuania, has left me confused.
Jewish, yes, but what about national flavor?
Recipes? What about wars? It's the Super Bowl today,
George will be gone for 12-24 hours, depending on who wins.
Still better than the way Vilnius switched hands.

Chickadees in the Mountain Ash

Let's collect agates from the canyon.
Let's forget the definition of beauty
and gather chips too little, too soft
to survive cuts and tumbles.

Let's fill our pockets
with smallness
simply because
we find it beneath our feet
at precisely the right time.
Let's lick rocks and not spit,
leave some for the birds.
Pick translucent
huckleberries with our teeth.

Let's choose the small ones
just because
there are so many.

Eleanor Leonne Bennett, photograph

Box of Rocks

Halfway beneath a table,
lid torn back,
$2 scrawled in black marker on the side,

these yard-sale rocks, heavy
as regret.

Two dollars, the price of an accumulation.

Scumbled with mud, collaged
in dry leaf, bits
of cobweb, the lost wings of insects,

they glint
like old loves, rugged stars.

They too had lives once,

arrived in this unlikely place
because someone spotted a moon in them

because a hand reached out and said, *You.*

O to have been the one chosen,
the hurried heartbeat of that.

Dimple, curvature, an angle
of polish. A palm that curled itself
around our shape,

and in its closing became our shape.

To have come through the tumbling.
And then, this hardness

we were shouldered into, the dismal
weight of us.

Lid folded down,
the cardboard darkness,

our hearts ticking, one against another.

Sam Joyner, photograph

Miranda in Naples

It's not the dresses
she hates most —
though after half

a lifetime of tropical sun
licking her back in afternoon
they fail to warm her

insides. It's the layers
of smallclothes underneath —
bleached smocks and bodices,

laced partlets, corsets, and girdles —
that make her wonder why
she ever settled for Ferdinand

and civilization. She refuses
to accept how colorless
garments make her feel:

as if she should not love
the flesh alive, beneath.
She tries to imagine what

the monster who first desired her
might say about her swaddled form —
but then remembers he never

used language to shape lack,
until she filled the space
between their bodies

with words that now
unbidden come into her mouth,
making it hard to breathe.

Dear University Office of Risk Management

Thank you for sending me a questionnaire about my dog. I suppose you learned about the animal from someone on my hall. I will refrain from asking whether it was Dr. Krystal Drum (Office 102) or Dr. Marcus Flaglatt (Office 104), respecting the importance of confidentiality in communication with your office. In the same vein, I have elected to leave the dog's name out of this missive. Nevertheless, I will tell you this in response to your queries about his or her bite history: I have taken steps to expunge from the record anything that might jeopardize the dog or the university, including the long ago birdbath debacle and the even more distant finger food snafu. In addition, it has been many years since any compromising incident might have been logged in official annals. Factor in the expansive quality of dog years (usually a seven-to-one ratio), and you will agree it has been over half a lifetime since any unpleasantness with the dog might have been documented. This circumstance is rather odd, as I first bought him or her as an attack animal. The dog (whose breed need not be disclosed but who is a massive specimen) was supposed to provide security. It was not walking the streets that bothered me so much as opening my apartment door, wondering if someone was inside burglarizing me or, worse still, lying in wait. Yet due to seizures the dog suffers from separation anxiety, it proves impractical to leave him or her alone to guard my property. Consequently, I always keep the dog close, even at work. Barring him or her from my office—as some of my colleagues might recommend—will cause me difficulty. This, in turn, might compromise my engagement with my work: a book-length study on monstrosity, which, Derrida posits, permits us to understand conventions by transgressing them. As such, your acceptance of the enclosed, blank questionnaire would be most appreciated.

Sincerely,

Dr. Noel Sloboda, Researcher in the Humanities

Encl. (1): questionnaire

Obfuscation

I went to the porch to pee in the pot,
child that I was and am.
It was the missing dog I stepped on,
some part of Freddie
under the quilt on the floor.

White porcelain pot
gray stitches in the quilt
sunrise in the windows.

No, my mother said, *impossible.*

One of many lies she told me.
I love her, liar, love her.
She will never leave me,
lie,
lie.

She will always —

bone-hard shining silver lie.

She Gives Me the Watch off her Arm

she wants me to
go to college

the closest she has ever been
is this
the dorm

her father had needed her
to dig the potatoes
and load them into burlap bags

for the train
but here she is
leaving her daughter

on the campus in the city time to go
we are at the desk
the clerk is wide-

eyed when my mother
asks her if she will
take an out-of-town check

if the need arises
if something comes up
so my girl will have money

even I know
this isn't going to happen
this check-cashing

a clerk helping me with money
but miracle of miracles
the clerk says nothing

and I say nothing
and my mother feels better
we go to the parking lot

old glasses thick dark hair
she is wearing a man's shirt
has to get back to the job

we stand beside her Ford and it is
here she undoes the buckle
of the watch and holds it out to me

my father's watch
keeping good time for him
and then for her

she says she knows I will
need a watch to get to class
we hug and she gets in

starts the car
eases into traffic
turns at the light

no wave
the metal
of the back of the watch

is smooth to my thumb
and it keeps for a moment
a warmth from her skin.

It Was a Game No One Taught Us

We used our hands to scrape together
a pile of dead grass; on our knees
we scrambled and gathered, our fingers raking
dry strands off their dry roots. We scraped
more, made a line of grass, made a corner, kept going,
made other corners, a square or rectangle, and we said

*this is the kitchen, this is the bedroom, here's the
door.* What we had was a blueprint,
a structure we could be alive in. *You're
in the spare room,* we said to one another,
or we said, *You just got home — take off your coat.*

In this way I lay a word
perpendicular to another, turn a
corner, make a string of words
to enclose something. I send
that enclosure to you:
what it keeps in, what it keeps out.

Best Order

A teacher once told me to hold a ruler like a razor

beneath my sentences—up to the jugular—a threat

to make them stranger, to see them for the first time

again and again, so I might find the flaws

and fix. As I look at you, as I have for most of the last decade,

through the bottom of my glass, through a bedsheet

of smoke, I understand—we must make each other

strange again each day. Even as the prying stars

peer in through the Venetians, we

must blind ourselves to that starshine of sameness

so we might see—vex ourselves once more

to venture a straighter line, a sentence that stabs and is kind.

Progeny

It is said that Keats wept upon waking
to discover he was still alive.
Blood in his lungs, two warped barrels
abrim with port. Can you imagine
the tableau: Severn at his side,
watching his chest rise
and fall like fortune, raking
a damp curl from his brow —
it would be snipped
after he rasped his last, bound
like a shock of tarnished wheat. I feel
as if I'm standing in a corner
of that dank last room, wondering
what I know: a relative
in calling only, who can't imagine
death's slow appraisal.
I hear the slick dribble of a rag
as it's bathed in cool water, held
uselessly to his dimming brow.
The bray of a cough that blooms
in the poet's mouth, a garden
of unwanted roses.
To call this sick boy
kindred, to know he bred ruin
in his chest like so many children
is a pang I'd like to thank him for.
If I had a veil I'd draw it
to hide my claret cheeks
as I tilt back in time
to bask in his last breaths.
I know only that Keats
heard history in birdsong
and wept for us — the still-here,
the eyes and too-full ears.

Crossing River

Sloshing interminably, water
up to his thighs, the hefty saint
carries the lost aloft, back and forth,
home
and destination.

In the middle of a night he pauses,
unburdened, in the middle of the river.
Snow is falling, disappearing like eyelashes
in the cold black stream

when the boatman drifts near,
oars quiet, rocking. The giant offers him a light
from his breast pocket, left by some traveler, who knows when.
They smoke.

The boat's lantern glows
a wavering pennant. Flakes flare
momentarily incandescent
before dissolving, becoming
more river.

Pretty night, says the boatman. *You ever feel the cold?*
The giant's head shakes. His beard sheds snow.
I'm used to it. You?
The boatman nods.
Don't much like rowing into wind, that's all.

A halloo from the shore. The giant turns.
Yours? Or mine?
Flip a coin—here, I've got plenty, says the boatman,
and then, *Never mind. You stay. I'll go this time.*
and the water runs around the giant's waiting thighs
and the boatman dips his oars

Missing Head

In the most beautiful part of the story
she finally finds
her sister's missing head.

It's on the far wall.
She climbs in through the window
and crosses the sooty floor.

She reaches up
and takes that face in her hands
the way you might lift a full bowl
of flowers down from a shelf, the moon
down from the cold part of the sky —

she wraps it in her cloak
and hurries away.

When she swims back to the boat
in the cold sea-dark
she holds the head up
so it won't get wet. She swims

side-stroke, what old folks swim
in dreamy laps in lakes in front of summer
cottages, another way to occupy

two worlds. I tested it once:
one arm raised all the way across the otherwise
deserted swimming pool

the imaginary head of my imaginary twin
held up, ready to be restored
when I got to the other side.

Deconstructing the Moon

She says "moon," and the word forms like a bubble,
hovering close to her lips. She thinks *lunar,*
luminous, and *round,* but those words do not appear.

She says the word "light," and the moon
moves across the patio, touches the table top,
smears the grass like a slow snail, before it silvers

the maple and climbs to the top of the pines,
where it breaks *like an egg yolk,* spilling color
down upon the tree, where it mixes with the odor

of the pines, and she thinks *dampness* and *dew,*
but she says nothing, and then the moon is gone.
She could have said, "cloud," thought *rain, haze,*

cumulous, but she did not, and then it was lost
behind a bank of evening clouds, and she could
not turn away, or it would become something else.

Natthimmel

Ytterst på ein avsats står det nokon
framfor eit tomt lerret
for å måle eit bilete av himmelen
like over midnatt
av himmelens tak og veggar
ståande på himmelens golv
i den mørkaste timen
dyppar penselen i mørkret
som kjem flytande inn

Han trekker opp konturane
til ei usynleg skisse
av himmelens mekanikk
eit system av utvekslingar
tannhjul og løftestenger

Himmelens innside, eit mekanisk underverk
frå ei tid då himmelen heldt opp med å eksistere
og det er dette han målar, med penselen
tung av flytande mørker, i den mørkaste timen
ytterst på ein avsats

Night Sky

Farthest out on a mountain ledge
he stands in front of an empty canvas
ready to paint a picture of the sky
just above midnight
of the sky's roof and walls
standing on the floor of the sky
in the darkest hour
he dips his brush into the darkness
that comes streaming in.

He outlines the contours
for an invisible sketch
of the sky's machinery
a system of reciprocating gears
cogwheels and levers —

the sky's interior, a mechanical miracle
from a time before the sky ceased to exist
and it's this he paints with his brush
heavy with the streaming darkness
in the darkest hour
farthest out on a mountain ledge.

Translated from the Norwegian by Damon Aukema

After You Died

I breathed

the long black sleeve of night
down my throat and pulled it
down my spine down my legs

closed my eyes and went under
the covers breathed it down
again and again as if its starry buttons

could stub a path to you

I kept breathing down the dark
'til morning came and every breath
hurt the more I breathed the more I kept

on breathing   I wanted to stop

as you had so beautifully
the wind clearing the way
for you to follow

like the silence you left behind
in which I am still trailing
the hems of your last breath

The Last Detail

There are any number of ways that Phil Swenson did not die.

He did not die of malaria, trichinosis, scarlet fever, yellow fever, typhoid fever, rabies, Ebola, or the plague.

He did not die of a 9mm bullet wound to the back of the head, the hot, abrasive grit of a remote African airstrip biting into his knees.

He did not die after a plunge from a 15th story Manhattan window, leaving all concerned to wonder whether he fell, leaped, or was pushed.

He did not die of exposure at 27,000 feet on the southwest ridge of Dhaulagiri as the long-awaited dawn began to color the icy peaks around him an astonishing, delicate red.

He was not shivved in the shower of a level-three men's correctional facility. He was not iced, hit, whacked, taken out, or bumped off. He was not fitted with a cement overcoat, pumped full of lead, or left to sleep with the fishes.

He died with a net worth of $273,310.18, a significant portion of which was a $250,000 life insurance policy whose main beneficiary remained his ex-wife, Gloria. His company, at the time of his death, continued to offer top-shelf health, vision, and dental plans.

Phil was not dismembered, detonated, dropped in a vat of industrial waste, seared by molten metal, dissolved in acid, or crushed in a stamping plant. He was not exsanguinated, disemboweled, or impaled.

At the time of his death, Gloria, who after the divorce moved to Phoenix, was working on her golf game. Chipping was still a problem for her, but as he died she laid a beauty up onto the notoriously tricky green of the 14th hole of the Buena Montana Country Club course. Yes, she thought, allowing herself a small fist pump. That's the way it's done.

No psychic or mystical events accompanied Phil's death. He was not borne aloft by angels. Demons did not rend his flesh. His body did not dissolve into a brilliant rainbow of light. His chakras remained closed. He transcended nothing. He did not spontaneously combust. He was not martyred for his beliefs.

His daughter, Patricia, who was twenty-one when Phil died, awakened 42 minutes after the fact—pried open her gummy eyes at 3:13 in the afternoon and stared blankly for a few moments at a poster taped to the wall opposite her. It was the stylized face of a handsome bearded man in a beret rendered in black on a red background. Jesus, she thought, Che Guevara. I should so be done fucking guys who have posters of Che Guevara. I've got to quit doing coke, she thought. Maybe a little pot on the weekends. And X for special occasions, but absolutely no more coke.

When Phil died, he had not attained the position of Vice President of Marketing at Altamont Systems. "Laura Alred doesn't know a market segment from a hole in the ground," people had agreed, filing into his office as if at a funeral. "You've been carrying her since she joined," they all had said, shaking their heads sadly before wandering off down the hall to where Laura was holding an impromptu party, accepting everyone's congratulations and giving the décor of her new office a serious rethinking.

Phil's son, Bob, two years younger than Patricia, was, at the time of his father's death, suffering through a particularly disappointing college football game. Despair filled Bob's heart as he watched the thoroughly mediocre opposing team rip off one big gainer after another. His jaw slack, he clutched at his hair as the hot autumn afternoon filled with a great collective groan. This is the worst thing, he thought. This is the very worst thing that could happen.

Phil did not meet his end at the hands of a jealous husband, or a jealous wife, girlfriend, or boyfriend. He was not the victim of a crime of passion. He did not die for love.

At Phil's funeral, Gloria sits at the front of the chapel taking stock of her feelings, because that seems to be what people are supposed to do at these things. The most prominent feeling, she thinks, is that of physical discomfort. Her toes are numb in her elegant black patent-leather heels. There seems to be a speck of something in her eye, which she dares not address lest the whole subtle edifice of shadow, liner, and mascara collapse around her. Her hair, which has been pulled back into a tight bun, the official hairstyle of grief, is tugging at her scalp in a way that almost certainly presages a throbbing hair headache.

But beyond all this, all the afflictions of prettiness, she realizes that there is another feeling, something hollow and sad behind her sternum, and she understands that this is the feeling of failure. Her adulthood, which had seemed as if it would be so effortless when she embarked on it, has gone terrifically wrong—a fact that, even now, seems inconceivable. She has, after all, kept her part of the bargain.

She married her high school sweetheart, the other half of the Cutest Couple. She gave birth to the requisite two beautiful children. She worked to be a good mother and wife.

But at each turn she was met with one disappointing revelation after another. That she and Phil, for example, had nothing in common besides good looks. That Phil, beyond the back-slapping, handsome-guy charm that he used to coast through life, wasn't particularly interesting. That her two children, whom she loved— loved in a fierce, I-will-never-be-whole-again way—have grown up to be strange, miserable young adults.

It was the car that did it. When Phil showed up with the Camaro, just a few weeks into Bob's junior year in high school, she knew she had to leave him.

She understands how it looks—especially to Patricia, who, it seems to Gloria, has spent her entire life examining her mother for hidden weaknesses—that she is flighty and shallow and stupid, just an aging beauty without the toughness required to get through the hard parts of life. She composes elaborate parables for them in her mind. "Think of a man and woman lost in the center of a great, black sea, many miles from land," she imagines saying to them, as they look at her with a wide-eyed, trusting wonder that she has not seen in many years. "The man begins to panic. He thrashes in the water and clutches at the woman as he would a life preserver, but his desperation threatens to pull them both down. The woman begins to feel her own fear rising as they go under again and again. Icy water fills her nose and mouth. Her breath, when she can fight her way back to the surface, comes in great, painful heaves. Can you understand that a woman in that situation might fight and kick her way free of the man's grasp? That such a woman might, even if she had promised to love that poor, drowning man forever, be forced to turn her back on him and swim away? And can you imagine the shame such a woman might feel, the terrible suspicion that she might be incapable of unconditional love?" But when she sees her children, the reality of what they are now, Bob with his air of confused sadness and Patricia all sharp edges and brittle cynicism, the words die in her mouth.

She knows that Patricia thinks that she has gone to a world of spectacular decadence—that she dines on the sautéed corpses of endangered animals and wades through great sewers of sex with poolboys and gigolos. She wonders what would happen if she told Patricia that she has a pretty-woman PR job with a chemical company. That she has gone out with three men since arriving in Phoenix. That each of them was a former success who had undergone some sort of dramatic personal implosion—bankruptcy, rehab, a narrowly escaped indictment for embezzlement. That these men seem to be the demographic left to aging beauties—she's too old to be a trophy but still too pretty for all but the most arrogant and self-absorbed.

A few weeks after she arrived, a giant dust storm had descended on the city, diverting airplanes and spawning countless Internet videos. She stood and watched it approach, a roiling brown cloud thousands of feet high, a ravenous tsunami of dirt devouring everything before it. It howled outside her condo for forty-five minutes, and afterwards everything—cars, lawns, buildings—was covered by a brown layer of grit, like cheap pancake makeup on an old woman. This is me, she thought. This is my life now.

In the men's bathroom at the funeral home, Phil's son Bob scowls into the mirror. Who is going to disrespect us in our house, he asks himself silently. He bares his teeth. *Who is the chump that is going to come in and disrespect us in our house?* That's more like it. He gives a little growl. He is starting to feel it. "Motherfucker," he whispers, "Motherfucker coming into our house, thinks he can diss us." He pauses, feeling fierce. "Motherrrrfuckerrr," he says, a little bit louder, drawing the syllables out. "Do NOT bring your raggedy ass in here and disrespect us in our house." He grasps the edge of the sink and leans into the mirror. "Motherfucker. Motherfucker. Motherfucker," louder and louder, over and over again until he is shouting at the top of his lungs.

The bathroom door swings open, and Steve, the mortuary guy, walks in, catching Bob in mid-shout. After a moment of confusion, Bob closes his mouth and runs some water over his hands as if he were washing them. A mistake, he sees, because he has spent the morning writing inspirational messages on his palms, and the ink is now blurring and running onto the white porcelain of the sink, making it appear as if Bob were losing large quantities of black blood.

Bob turns the water off and Steve wordlessly hands him a paper towel, which just makes things worse.

"I thought . . ." Steve finally says, "I thought I heard something."

Bob takes a brief glance at his right palm. "Failing to prepare is preparing to fail." He can still make that out, written near the wrist, but everything else is just a blur. He tries to think of some of the other ones. "Winning isn't everything—it's the only thing." That was one of them.

"I was just . . ." Bob begins. A long pause follows.

"Yeah," Steve finally says. "OK. I'll be outside if you need me."

Patricia stands in the lobby, attempting to make a phone call. The cell phone buzzes its thin sibilance in her ear. It sounds like a drill, she thinks. How has she never noticed before how much it sounds like a drill, some sort of heavy-duty industrial thing augering its way into her skull.

Pick up, Derek, she thinks. Pick up the fucking phone. Her skin feels like a tight plastic membrane, as if she has been shrink-wrapped in her own body. Her head throbs.

"Patricia, the service is about to start. Who are you calling?" Patricia jumps, her heart racing even faster than before. She wonders how her mother crept up on her so quietly.

"Nobody," Patricia says, quickly hanging up. Realizing how stupid that must have sounded, she then blurts out "Derek." Which is the last thing she wanted to say. There is really no reason anybody has to know that she was calling Derek.

Her mother arches her perfect brows in surprise. "Derek? You're calling Derek? Why are you calling Derek?"

Patricia rolls her eyes. This is why she keeps secrets: she is surrounded by people who become insane over the tiniest little things.

"He said, you know..." she pauses. She tries to choose her words carefully but realizes that she has entered The Zone of Unintentional Frankness, a place more and more familiar to her these days, where the normal checks and balances between her brain and her mouth don't work quite as well as she might wish. "I wanted him to come."

"Derek? To your father's funeral? Your father hated Derek."

Patricia turns away from her mother's calculating stare. She thinks about going into the bathroom for a quick bump out of the Secret Stash, but then remembers that the Secret Stash is empty, that all of that coke that should have lasted until, well, forever, since she doesn't do coke anymore, had melted mysteriously away, which, if she were completely honest, was one tiny reason, one among many, that she was calling Derek, because Derek always had coke. But if any circumstances justified—demanded, really— dipping into the Secret Stash—well, OK, consuming the entirety of the Secret Stash and then calling Derek to see if she could get some more—it had to be now, her father's funeral, with her mother squeezed into that tight black skirt designed to show everyone that she still had her fabulous ass, and her brother Bobby looking red-eyed and strange, with some black shit on his hands that she didn't have the energy to ask about, and the chapel being almost empty, like her dad didn't even have any friends, though that couldn't have been right because he was really a good guy. And her stand-ing just outside, in the lobby of this horrible little funeral home with the cheap hi-wear carpet that is so stiff and harsh she can feel every little bump and nubbin of it through her shoes, and the oily funeral home guy with his lacquered-on, second-hand grief, and the organ groaning away inside like the haunting moans of the dead and the dim light shining through the crappy pseudo-stained glass windows that are really just colored pebbled plastic sheets covering fluorescent-lit alcoves to create a thin simulation of the sun coming through . . . the whole thing is completely intolerable. So much worse than she could have imagined. Anybody would dip into the Secret Stash under those conditions. Anybody. The Dalai fucking Lama himself would be on the Secret Stash like a fifteen-horsepower shop vac if he were here in this awful place, getting ready to put her father into the ground.

Patricia stares at her mother, speechless. Her mouth, which, just a few moments ago, had been completely happy to babble unnecessary things about Derek, had decided to go on break. Patricia thinks that it would be an excellent time to set a few things straight, to make it clear that the moral high ground is entirely hers. It was, after all, her mother who had abandoned the three of them, moving to glamorous Phoenix and leaving them to. . .well, it was hard to describe what had happened to all of them. In her head, she composes wave after wave of devastating verbal attacks that will leave her mother in remorseful tears, begging Patricia for forgiveness, but her mouth remains stupidly and stubbornly shut. Finally her thumb decides to take matters into its own hands by hitting the redial button on her phone. Patricia brushes angrily past Gloria and into the bathroom as the industrial-drill ringing begins again.

Bob lurches into the lobby and catches sight of his mother, who is staring at the door of the women's bathroom with a defeated expression on her face. Even in her severe black funeral-type dress she is terrifically beautiful. He wants to run to her, to bury his head in her lap, to feel her warm arms around him. He wants her to murmur softly into his ear. He wants her to make everything all right.

She turns and their eyes meet, and she gives him a small, tentative smile. He has to unburden himself, to tell her about the dead emptiness that has taken up residence in his chest. He opens his mouth and says, "Nine and three isn't good enough."

"What?"

He knows he has confused her, but he can't think of anything else to say. "State, I mean. The football team. We've already got three losses. The best we can do is nine and three. We were ranked at the beginning of the season, and now we've already got three losses."

She looks at him with kindness, and he feels a brief moment of hope. "Bob," she says gently, "can we talk about something other than sports for once? Can't this all wait until after the funeral?"

And he wants to say no, no, no, it can't wait. He knows what she thinks—that a football loss is just hung-over, shame-faced eighteen-year-old boys who have painted themselves entirely green, stadium bathrooms overflowing with vomit and urine, sullen, drunken fistfights in the parking lot, 60,000 people in a fog of common despair. And it's true. Nine and three does look a lot like that, but it's so much more. Nine and three is shattered expectations, ruin and despair. It's blackness and anguish and the dissolution of all things, inconsolable misery, the death of love. He looks at her wildly, trying to think of a way to tell her this. Nine and three is his mother moving to Phoenix, and his sister the cokehead, and his father. . .he can't even begin to think about his father. He takes a trembling breath. "Nine and three doesn't even get you into the conversation," he says. "There's no way nine and three gets you to the dance." Her eyes are full of tears now. He sees in her a deep, motionless sadness and feels a strange, unbidden joy arise. She knows, he thinks. For a moment he is not alone. "Pain is temporary, but victory is forever," he says in a rush. That one, he remembers now, was on his left thumb. There is a long silence, and then his mother touches him gently on the cheek and looks away.

Gloria, having failed again with both of her children, turns from her son and pulls open the door to the chapel. As she walks up the central aisle, a disturbing feeling of familiarity fills her. This is, she realizes, just like her wedding day—the elaborate makeup, the beautiful but torturous shoes, walking toward Phil—or whatever is left of him—with the sense that each step is portentous, irrevocable, final.

When she was young, she often fancied herself the heroine of one of those animated movies where, in the final frames, the handsome stable boy is revealed to be a noble prince, and, as the couple kisses for the first time, woodland creatures gambol around them in ecstatic song.

She tries to summon them to her now, those cartoon bluebirds and squirrels and rabbits and anthropomorphic raccoons. Come on, she thinks. You started this. Don't leave me now. Sing to me of rigor mortis and formaldehyde, of probate court and estate taxes. Follow me through my life as you once promised to do. Serenade me with gay songs of cataracts and osteoporosis, prolapsed rectums, dementia and blood clots, of catheters and incontinence. Hey, little animals, she thinks, looking around the chapel and finding no comfort there, this is your cue. It's time for you to do your job.

In the bathroom, Patricia hits redial on her phone one more time. She takes deep, shaky breaths to compose herself as the horrible industrial ringing sound again bites into her ear, and she starts to think that, in spite of everything, in spite of the fact that her father had, actually, really sort of hated him, it would be wonderful if Derek showed up. It would be one more person in that empty chapel, one more final little beacon of love for her father, and it would show everyone what a good and generous man he was. That he was willing to forgive anything. It is, she realizes, very important that Derek show up. For her father. When her call rolls over to his voicemail, she says, in a voice that sounds dry and tense even to her, "Derek. It's Patricia. Get over here. Right now." She puts the phone back in her purse and looks at herself in the mirror. Her eyes are red and her hands shake slightly. Which, in reflection, is fine. It is only appropriate that there should be some signs of physical distress in the mourners.

She leaves the bathroom and enters the chapel. Everybody is already seated, her mother and brother in the front row. She is the very last person in, and it feels as though everyone stares sullenly at her as she walks by, as though they had all been waiting for hours, days, years for her to finally show. The chapel is so quiet she can hear the brush of her nylons as she walks, and the soft crunch of her feet on those unyielding nylon carpet fibers. She can hear the rhythmic, pneumatic workings of people's lungs, the great bellows of a life that her father had abandoned. She sits next to Bob and her mother and tries to avoid looking at the coffin, a glossy, aggressive oak thing that manages to look simultaneously modern and antique, like an escape pod from a Victorian starship. The minister rustles some papers at the lectern, a sound like the flapping wings of carrion birds. He clears his throat and opens his mouth to speak, and just then, Patricia's phone goes off. "It's raining men," it sings joyously through its tinny, demonic little speaker. "Hallelujah, it's raining men."

At the time of his death, Phil was waxing his 1978 Camaro in the driveway of his 3,600-square-foot suburban ranch home. High blood pressure caused a vessel near the hypoglossal canal in Phil's brain to burst. He was suddenly overcome by exhaustion and collapsed slowly to the ground. His head lolling loosely, he saw a bulbous reflection of his face in the curve of the mirror-waxed fender. He was not enveloped in a brilliant, loving white light. His life did not pass before his eyes. He did not think of the summer after his high school graduation, when, shirtless, he would spend every Saturday detailing an automobile nearly identical to this one, of how sometimes girls would drive by slowly just for the breathless pleasure of seeing him there—Phil and his lean, tan body working away at the gleaming red finish of that fabulous muscle car—185 horses in a 350 V8, six-speed short-throw performance shifter, four-barrel carb. He did not think of those days when the universe seemed to open up before him like a long, bright highway, of the feeling of rocketing faster and faster into the limitless future, top down, foot to the floor.

Elegiac Variations on Yes, We Have No Bananas

He introduces it after the *Dies Irae* (in *vox humana*),
certain that no one will recognize the tune: not the priest
(too unworldly), not the handful of mourners
(all immigrants), not the altar boys (half asleep).

At the offertory he offers pastoral variations
(for piccolo and oboe) and at the *Ite, missa est*
a sweeping inversion (*à la* his beloved Sergei).
And when the casket is wheeled out (head toward

the door) he pulls out all the stops (a *Grand
Polonaise Brillante!*) abandoning it (and the loft)
as soon as the old men in their painful suits
sidle out to see what the day will bring.

Being the Violin, for Gaspara Stampa, Venetian Poet and Singer c. 1550

Allegro: capillaries
of light fretting
Collatino's creeks. Lento:
nightfall eclipsing
the junipers in rows
like blue-black torches
on the Isle of Bones.

The idea of being the violin
didn't come at once.

The wood began it,
remembering the trees—
the stomach's just perceptible
swelling with April sap;
the f-shaped sound hole
summer thickened
to darken and deepen
soprano to contralto.

The buds compressed
in their sheaths,
the bole's arch and bend
in wind, ice of winter's desire
to abide, enter the violin's keening,

and the strings taut with a cat's
wild fear, notes
so high they hurt below
each ear. Then the mourning
bass resonates in the chest
and brings closure
to allegro, pizzicato.

The pressure on frets, the bow
arm working like a hollow wing,
and inside, resonant
rosewoods of shadow
like the Count's old blood:
now I'm the music
making light
of desire.

Shoshana Kertesz, photograph

Unsexing Them

They were not meant to be lovers. I realize this
after writing more than two hundred pages
and at first I try to deny it, but of course it is true.
It isn't a story about an affair. Victor is as faithful
to his wife as a gold filling, and Simone's passion
for painting leaves no room for a lesser love.
And so I begin unsexing them.

With Yankee thrift, I cut the sex scenes
into a new file (waste not, want not), beginning
at the end of the manuscript. First, I remove
their final night together, more loss than lust, the sheets
damp with tears and sweat, Simone's dream of the boat
in a wild sea, the words *heavy* and *hidden*, *hollow* and *bite*.

Deleted: the night they meet by chance at the train station,
their hurried union bent over the sink in the narrow bathroom.
A few keystrokes and the scene is nothing but a way to flee Boulogne.
Stolen goes, but *railway* stays; I take *longing* and leave *furlong*.
I remove how the quick sharp pain of him thrills her, I remove
how earlier they had fallen together on the carpet in the coldwater flat,
his scraped knee, the bruise on her elbow, the taste of sauternes
on his tongue, the word *stunned*. I remove the words *shallow* and *sate*,
sudden and *slow*.

Last to go, the weekend in the country (Victor's wife in the garden
pulling lupine; Simone's canvas wet in the hot shed), their first time,
the paragraphs green with discovery, raw, each noun *hunger*,
each adjective *insatiable*, drowsing afterward in the bee-buzzing field,
her bare arm swagging his bare chest, the tall grasses flattened
around them like the blast radius of a bomb, the slight breeze
whispering over them, picking up its chill
from the surface of the dark lake.

They walk through the edited white pages guileless
as unpainted wood, smiling at each other without a lilt
of hidden pleasure. Their affection for each other is obvious
and bald as a well-lit kitchen, nearly familial. Paragraph after paragraph
of *sunlit cotton, blue and yellow pigments, solace* and *sorrow* and *bread*.

Yet through it all—through Simone packing her suitcase full of sketches,
the fighting in the Ardennes, Victor handing his wife the silver cup—
their other life unfolds across seventeen patchwork pages buried in a subdirectory,
not wearing a stitch of plot, throwing continuity to the wind, the whole
of its story nothing beyond pulse, tongue, throat, and thigh.
Page after page of *surreptitious*, *sweetness*; *furtive* following *flesh*,
release following *ravishment*, line after line of *lingering, lightly, love*.

Sheldon Tapley, "Bacchanal," oil on panel

Held by five nerves, your tongue verges on fire

Your tongue speaks better as pencil.
The graphite roots, the molten cloud.
The syllables escaping — —   black vibrations.

Kali wanted the world charcoal so even fire would know its burn.

In smoke, the roots of speech simmer as a red vine. There's even a six-

fingered hand pushing thought forward. (That extra   finger
                                    which got chopped
            off to make a girl.) In the roots, a calendula

growing, unseen thorns twisted like blood
                        inside out.

Kali prefers an endpoint, that full stop you dotted
the page with, that attempt to make the thought close — —

        You fear absorption — —black palate stretching. A now, no
                                            longer.

You write: I crossed the bridge. I bridged.

Shave pencil: volcano oozes. Reach into middle earth,
            where the nerves end in a calendula growing.

        In the dark there is no destiny — —   only movement.

Pierino Sempio

Tal vez fue la manera que tenías
de abrirlos,
de sostenerlos con la mano
frente al grupo
y caminar por el salón leyendo
con voz pausada,
sin dar explicaciones para no romper
el ritmo del relato,
como si el ritmo fuera todo,
aún más que el hilo de la historia
(la mano libre que guardabas
en el bolsillo de los pantalones te servía
para voltear las hojas
y, de paso, reconvenir
golpeándolo en la nuca
a alguno que no oía —
después volvías a hundirla
en esa parte de tu traje,
el único que usaste en toda la primaria),
lo que me descubrió cómo los libros
nos dan una postura,
una respiración distintas,
y escribo, más que nada,
para que un día los míos
se puedan sostener con una mano,
como sostenías los tuyos,
y sean legibles caminando,
la mano libre descansando en el bolsillo
y algo más libre descansando en uno
para poder seguir el hilo de la historia.

Pierino Sempio

Maybe it was your way
of opening them,
of holding them in your hand
in front of the group
and walking around the room reading
in a deliberate voice
without giving explanation so as not to break
the story's rhythm,
as if it were everything,
even more than the thread of the story
(the free hand tucked
in the pocket of your trousers
served to turn pages
and, in passing,
slap the back of the neck
of someone not listening–
after you once more shoved it
into that part of your suit,
the only one you wore throughout primary school);
you showed me how books
give us a posture,
a different way of breathing,
and I write, more than anything,
so that one day mine
can be held with a hand
the way you held yours,
and be legible walking,
the free hand resting in the pocket,
and something freer resting in oneself
so as to follow the thread of the story.

Translated from the Spanish by Kathleen Snodgrass

Nos recibía la casa a oscuras

Nos recibía la casa a oscuras
y andábamos a tientas los primeros días.
En el verano
la luz que apenas se trasmina
por las persianas de madera
es suficiente para andar por casa
y guarda la frescura de los cuartos.
De noche rara vez nos alumbraba un foco,
era de luz aún cuando nos recogíamos
y cada día, en la mañana,
abríamos una ranura nueva
y, gota a gota, el suero de la luz
desentumía la casa,
 hacía crujir los muebles,
restablecía la suspensión del polvo.
Con una casa a oscuras tantos meses
se oye cómo sus muros se vertebran
al recibir los rayos que se filtran,
reacostumbrándose a la casa que revive,
y todos los crujidos son
crujidos de convalescencia,
hasta que un día,
con un tronido seco y lúgubre
que bien podía venir de los cimientos
o aun de más abajo, de un abajo
que daba escalofrío,
se despedían todos los ecos
y esa noche,
llenos de envidia los vecinos
se detenían junto a la verja
de nuestra casa iluminada.

The house welcomed us in darkness

The house welcomed us in darkness
and the first couple of days
we made our way tentatively.
In summer
the light that weakly filters through
wooden shutters
is enough for walking around the house
and keeps the rooms cool.
Only occasionally at night did a bulb illuminate us;
it was still light when we went to bed,
and every day, mornings,
we opened a new slot;
drop by drop the whey of light
eased the house,
set the furniture creaking,
restored the suspension of dust.
With a house in darkness so many months
you could hear how the walls were built
to welcome the rays that penetrate,
how they realigned themselves with the house that revives,
and all the creaks
are creaks of convalescence,
until one day,
with a dry and lugubrious groan
that could well rise from the foundations
or even further down, so far down
it makes me shiver,
all the echoes and that night
said goodbye;
filled with envy, the neighbors
lingered near the fence
of our illuminated house.

Translated from the Spanish by Kathleen Snodgrass

Burning House

Because the place was long abandoned, rumored
haunted, and because they all stood at the threshold
between winter and spring, some mornings
almost warm, or at least back-lit in yellow light

the color of the sunflower fields that would,
any day now, rise up, shake the snow drifts off their
thin shoulders, it was cause more for celebration
than alarm. No one knew how the first flame caught—

the spontaneous combustion of old newspapers,
perhaps, or a pinpoint light burned into the dusty arm
of an antique chair, some old beauty waiting
to burn again, or the air oiled by a broken gas line

sparked by a rogue wire in the thin walls.
But when the firetruck's siren sounded, lightning-voiced
through the street, the people stumbled out, blinking their eyes,
brought thermoses and bundled babies who pointed

toward the flames. They nodded, *Yes, Yes—Fire,*
to the babies, to each other, smiling into the glitter-
rush melting away the snow, the water-stream rising
into a fine cloud of vapor above the ruin, above

the children dancing up to touch the cold water, delighted
by the sudden arrival of heat, their gray days turned
August. Soon, they knew, soon, they would run out into
those fields beyond the flames, hunch down in the brush

to hide from each other, to strike the matches
they stole from their mother's purses to make small fires
from tinder, old feathers, the dried bodies of crickets,
small as secrets, let them burn in the palms of their hands.

Horsefly

Grind down the gravel drive, its bristling dust
will scratch the window-cracks and engine rust—
and its white tongue can cut an eye. Hold hard
to the door. Our black sedan will rock and pitch
and the weeds that flower in the drainage ditch
are sickly pale, and the heat lords over the yard.

Out in the insect noise, our mothers swat,
but water lies beneath a wooden deck—
a dug-out pond that deepens to the neck,
where algae loosely swamp around the shores,
and we will swim, as my mother talks to yours
by citronella light, flames low and squat.
—"That man, for what he's worth, was all she had."
The dock is groaning, gray and white.
                                        —"So sad."
Fall hard and heavy to the water. Dive.
Come to the surface with burning eyes.
                                        —"She'll live."
Cattails knock in the wind. "With him or not."

then: *Horsefly, Horsefly!* —
                        a diving,
                        a static moan—
a vanishing, swerving close—all verve and drone—
and even though we've only seen the welt
on others' arms, and never on our own,
we know to fear what pain we haven't known,
to flinch before the bite we've never felt.

So we dive,
        we dive—
then night, dark-deep and wide,
floods over us and we cannot breathe, we ache:
the horsefly stalks on the surface of the lake.

We know there's only so long we can hide.

Original Sin

Born to a snake-bit house, I learned to fear
the Lord our God, whose hand is merciless —
      and there are numbers hung on every door.
      Don't tell me what to hope for anymore.

I can feel the grand finale drawing near
in billowing swells of smoke and steam: when loss
      lingers just outside the door and waits,
      watching you clear the table of the plates,

when florists take their flowers in for the night,
and the lampshade hides a dead cicada's husk;
      when we're set suffering for our own good,
      and there is no such thing as childhood

and there's no dream — just frail, eternal dusk:
Skies purpled like thumbnails as a lidless light
      bleeds from every corner, shop and car:
      Out on the asphalt roof, I see no star.

Cracked in the sink, a teacup leaks its tea —
what was left over, what was left behind —
      and we have watched the towers burning, we
      have seen the wind-swept bodies falling free —

yet we are left repeating what we're told:
There's nothing here to see. Time yawns, like cold
      bones ache before an empty fireplace.
      Love, I alone will look you in the face

as I array our kindling for the flame,
and I alone can tell you why you came —
      There will be nothing left but ash and bone,
      dark and dawn, the ocean and a stone —

but our silence is a bandage, raveled and sheer.
You face the future, lonely with your fear —
    the glaciers melting toward the marriage bed.
    There is always what one could have said

to haunt us, always how it might have been,
the mystery that was — and wasn't — seen,
    but there was no one left who did not fall,
    not knowing how to pray for once, for all.

We lost our tongues as horror rose with glory —
a colossal, chiseled stone. Down came our fury,
    and gracelessness grew brave, a kick and bray —.
    Once there was a clear September day

when we all faced the end to our own story:
We took our seats on that small, shadowed ferry,
    then ate our apples, swallowing the bite
    that left the bare flesh gleaming in the light.

Samantha Jones, photograph

Widowed Eve

She smokes alone outside,
watching the sun burn

a strip of red before
it slips from sight.

She can still conjure
Seth quiet in her arms,

Abel's red face crumpled
in his first cries, Cain, hungry,

chewing his own soft fist, even
Adam the morning she first rose,

his doubt that she could come
from his own aching rib.

But the face of God is gone.
The angels don't come anymore,

not even on moonless nights
when bright Sirius glows

like a cigarette between
curtains imperfectly hung,

imperfectly closed.

About J. Robert Oppenheimer

Though he walked in Einstein's shadow,
he could see the faint outlines of another
story. He sat at the master's feet,
gathered the gleanings of dust
from the floor, sifted them through
his porous hands, looked for kernels
of gold shining from the bottomless pit.
Then the mandate to build the bomb,
and his world of spectatorship came
to an end. He embraced the powers
given him by his mentor, harnessed
energies not of his own making,
and built death into a palpable thing.

*Now I am become Death, destroyer
of worlds*, he thought, mumbling
the Hindu text as if he were *davening*
in *shul* at the eastern wall though
the end of the war was visible through
the mushroom cloud. Later, enemies
charged him with nothing short of treason,
but he knew in the pulsing space between
his veins what Adam must have known
when, having eaten sweet fruit of the Tree
of Knowledge and having been driven out
of timeless Eden, he was told by Almighty
God that this is life and this is death.

Alentejo

A south wind
tousles the leaves
of the Azinheira tree
beyond our bedroom window—
even the ants are startled
by a momentary sunlight.
Twenty years ago, in Lisbon,
I stumbled down from the Coliseu
toward the Tejo.
The lights of the Praça do Comércio
were flares you could cup in your hands.

The decades amass,
but the past is ever-vivid:
an icing of clouds above the Alentejo,
the bleat of sheep
from a hillside across the valley.
I never leave it.
I sing it to myself again and again.
It has become a testament,
the song that created the world.

In Pagan Fashion

When centuries were fewer
and Sygtrygg sailed the Seine

in red feathers and spinals
dream adorned man.

The chimera of time
beat by evening's molten leaves.

The sun lone and divine
the moon nude in the dark.

The pungent smell of chance
sprinkled over seas and rivers.

Rocks and trees muttered to,
around whose mossy monuments

amber, love, immortal victory were
cradled by the amorphous fog.

Tomorrow ambushed with an axe
and the clear unflinching eyes.

Yesterday magnified and pinned
like a butterfly's dazzle.

Void of intemperate innocence
lewd transgressions,

wine's fair locks
humble benches cornering warmth.

Flesh in the guise of milk, clay
a ruddy cheek, spiraled gold.

For me too the belief
that lost things return,

the faultless intimacy that dwells in spirit,
the practical law of transmigration.

Family History

i.

my grandmother was a bird
in Thessaloniki

she flew through open windows
she built beautiful nests
over the bare heads
of her village

no one could touch a feather

until her father
sat at the kitchen table
with a stranger

a bottle of rakiya between them

and let the stranger trap her
in a basket
all darkness

twice she slipped the lid
open
and flew home

the third time, the man
clipped her wings
tied her talon to the saddle

she remembered Persephone
who didn't want
to die

Eurydice who didn't want
to come back
to life

(or was it the other way around?)

she cooked his meals
washed road dust
from his shirts

raised four children
screech softening

no one guessed
that two of the children
had been born
with feathers on their backs

as though
they might one day
spread their arms
and fly

ii.

too many details are missing
for instance
what type of bird
the color of her feathers

for instance
the direction of the wind
the length of her shadow

was it summer was the moon full

what her mother said
when she flew back home
slipping through the open window

and which window
the kitchen or the bedroom
where her sisters slept

what her father said
to the man
when he made her go

for instance
a songbird or a bird of prey

for instance
a crow

I say she was a raven
who swallowed the world's light
and coughed it out
into the sun
and moon

I say her father was the thief
who locked the light
in a tiny box

locked within other boxes
each consecutively bigger
until they contained the world

I say the marriage
was her punishment
for breaking them open
one by one

feathers rising
and falling
wings
all starlight
beneath the lids

Water for Thieves

When the door creaked open, Elsa dug her head deeper into the pillow. She listened as her husband undid the watch from his wrist, then, her head turned, saw him kicking off his shoes and socks, coins falling onto the rug. His body shadowed toward the bed and his hand disappeared inside his jacket. He pulled out something shaped like a book and fell onto the mattress.

Later, as morning light inched its way toward her, Elsa saw the icon of St. Christopher, wild-eyed and yellow-haloed, sitting on the dresser.

"You stole it?"

He sat up, nodded, then cracked his knuckles.

"Take it back." She got up to take a closer look. Saint Christopher, naked from above the waist, stood beside a river, his ribcage etched with dark lines, his sapphire eyes glinting. The saint carried Jesus, a man-child in red, on one shoulder.

Her husband laughed, raked his fingers through his hair. It was not the first thing he had stolen. He had grabbed tomatoes from neighbors' gardens, lifted wine glasses left on balcony rails, secured bullets from the little museum in a neighboring town, relics from the war. Neighbors would check the bathroom after he visited for missing porcelain soap dishes. But he had never before stolen from a church.

The icon had a story. The Germans had marched through the Peloponnese over a quarter-century ago, setting fire to house after house, 'til, in the village, a bearded man had pleaded with the soldiers to stop. He had claimed there was no one left there but old women and goats, no reason to destroy abandoned houses. When the villagers returned, a girl asked a soldier why their houses had been spared. In muddled Greek, the soldier had answered, "We were told not to, by the man with a beard." "What man?" the girl said. "The man in the picture," he said, and pointed to an icon of St. Christopher on the front door of the church. Christopher took human form on that day, the villagers said, to dupe the Germans.

"It's a goddamn fable." Nico rubbed his bare chest. He got out of bed and smoothed out his wrinkled trousers.

"So what?" she said. The priest will be looking for you. Get rid of it." She began to put on a sleeveless dress.

With his foot, he slid the icon under the bed. It knocked against the high heels Elsa wore now only in the city, where they lived from fall to spring, in the seasons when he drove a cab. They returned to the village in the summers to gain distance from tourists and city heat.

"I can't take it back."

"You could have taken any of them," she said. "Some have enormous halos—gold and silver frames. You had to take *that* one."

"The church will buy another fucking icon. It's good for the economy."

"Did anyone see you? Altar boys?"

"Just the goats."

"Your father would wring your neck," she said. "If he knew."

On the wall hung portraits of Nico's father and grandfather, men who were not thieves, farmers who pursed their lips and considered the consequences of being photographed. There, too, was Elsa's mother, or at least the woman who had raised her. She had been childless till she rescued Elsa from the inside of a bus tire, an orphan lost in war.

"Enough," he said. "The first chance I get, I'll sell it."

She walked from the bedroom side of the room to the kitchen, one large space divided only by function. She opened the refrigerator and took out a bottle of goat's milk. She undid the plastic wrap on the lid as flies landed on the counter.

"We have no meat."

"Tragedy."

"What am I supposed to make for dinner?"

"You eat like a hummingbird. What difference does it make?"

"I was going to invite your mother. To prove we have nothing to hide."

Nico reached out and tried to catch a fly as Elsa spooned out some coffee. She reminded him of the chores, that the front door needed to be painted. The sound of a car muffler floated through the open window. She could hear boys pushing their creaky bicycles across the street, heard voices resurrecting last night's soccer game and the laments of the Regime of the Colonels. When the news of the missing icon filtered through the lace curtains, she gave Nico a withering stare. The housekeeper of the monastery had noticed the white space where it once hung and had grabbed a mop in case the thief was still under the monastery's roof. From down the street a bus appeared, and the voices in the distance grew faint.

"I'm thirsty." Nico put on a half-ironed shirt.

From the kitchen window Elsa watched him walk across the street to the cafenion to get his own coffee, to spend money they didn't have on katayifi and fried dough with honey. As the sun poured down, other men joined him under the awning at the cafe and sipped on orange sodas. Gossip of the possible thief floated around the card tables—gypsies from up north or a priest from a neighboring town who harbored a grudge against St. Christopher.

Elsa, immune to thirst, whacked flies on the window pane.

Rain had not come all summer. She could see the cracks in the dirt, on her hands. Faucets had slowed to mere drips. Only a few cisterns in the village still allowed the villagers to wash their blouses and boil potatoes.

Nico's pale yellow cab was parked on the street, the keys locked inside, bridesmaids' dresses in the backseat. A tuxedo hung against the passenger's side window. Elsa called out to him, and he finally wandered back, eating the last bite of a dolmada. He was supposed to have left the cab in Athens. His boss was probably cursing him, hiring an Albanian replacement.

She walked outside to meet him with a wire hanger. "Here."

She tilted her head at the cab and he peered at the keys in the ignition. She had sewing to do, alterations for a wedding, for a couple in Athens. Her sewing kit sat in the footwell in the backseat.

He unbent the hanger into a long piece of wire and made the end into a hook. He eased it into the top of the driver's side window. The muscles in his neck tightened and he swore.

She folded her arms. "If you've dropped any hints about your latest looting," she whispered, "bragging to those lazy card players, I'll drown you."

A widow, Anastasia Panusi, walked by and scrutinized the cab's contents. She adjusted her wire-rimmed glasses.

"Those dresses are going to turn yellow in the sun."

"It's locked."

"Who's getting married?"

"The groom's an engineer in Athens."

The widow glanced at Nico's untucked shirt, then at Elsa. "Maybe you should have married him."

Nico dropped the hanger and shot the woman a glare.

"I'll keep that in mind for next time," Elsa said.

As the widow walked away he cursed her under his breath. "You should have spit on her."

"Why don't you go steal her china?"

She saw the wounded look in his eye, as if he were a boy taunted in the schoolyard.

Inside the house, she searched for the extra car key in the sewing machine drawer and behind the upholstered chair whose cushion was split down the middle. No luck. Nico ran his hands across her back, located her neck under her hair.

"Not now," she said.

In bed the story was different. He began stroking her stomach, and she folded her legs around his. He brushed his oily hair against her neck, his turquoise ring rapping against the headboard. The mirror hanging in front of the armoire reflected the curtains suspended in the breeze. Afterwards, she found herself on his side of the bed and, mouth against the pillow, stared for the longest time at the wrinkles in the sheets.

"Gypsies used to read beds, like tea leaves."

"What?" Half-asleep, Nico stroked her rib cage and dangled his leg off the mattress, a regular habit, perhaps climbing monastery walls in his sleep.

Elsa folded back the top sheet and looked at the wrinkles and shadows, the imprint of bodies trying to stay in love. Nico mocked her sudden superstition. She got on her hands and knees and removed the icon from beneath the bed and held it up to a shaft of sunlight. The Christ child held a scroll that covered part of the saint's staff, a rod outlined in gold.

"That thing's worth a whole motorcycle." Nico mumbled into the mattress.

"I'm not riding on the back of a motorcycle."

His arm dropped to the floor, knuckles hitting hardwood.

"You can't sell this," she said. "They'll drown you."

"I thought *you* were going to drown me."

"I need the water for lemonade."

He lifted his head. "I can't keep up with you," he said. She noticed the line of his razor at the nape of his neck.

St. Christopher's jeweled irises sparkled beneath the halo of molten gold around his ring of curls. "Too bad he turned himself into a dog," she said. Villagers had said that Christopher was so handsome that women threw themselves at his front door. He did not want to be tempted, so he asked God to give him the face of a dog.

"I bet that didn't work," he said. "Women like dogs, too."

A truck drove past their window and catapulted sounds into the corners of the room.

"I'm tired of old women praying to dead men," he said. "No wonder the rest of the world is beyond us, Germany and England and — They have elevators that take you eighty stories up."

"If they come looking for you, they'll come looking for me."

"Well then you had better pray to Spiridon and Sebastian and Haralambos and all those other useless pricks who did nothing but trip over a hoe on Good Friday and ended up famous. What are they doing painted on the inside of church domes?"

❊ ❊ ❊

The town priest traveled from church to church in neighboring towns, asking cantors and ushers if they had seen the missing relic. Boys in town shared a single pair of binoculars and looked for any sign of a gypsy or stranger. An old woman, stooped-shouldered, monitored the remaining icons — Saint Joanna, Saint Joachim of Ithaca, and Theophanes the Branded — 'til sunset, then welcomed two girls who shared her watch. When the priest knocked on their door, Elsa answered. No, she hadn't seen the icon, but for the sake of appearances — and as a respite from Nico and the heat — she agreed to take on a shift at the monastery.

In the mornings, the women who shared her shift complained of their aching muscles and lamented the disappearing youth in the village, girls and boys who'd found other lives in Athens and cared nothing for churches and saviors. Elsa was unlike the women who had never left the village and unlike those who had never come back. She lived between. When in Athens, she dreamed of walking the donkey beneath the almond trees after rain. When in the village, she thought only of the Plaka and the refined men in Italian suits who descended elevators, the bright packaging and ribbons in the store windows.

Together, the women on duty gathered before the space where the icon was missing. One of them reached out a hand to

Elsa. They touched fingers as Elsa's eyes fell on the icon next to the blank space, a painting of the Virgin and Child. The Christ child's hand was placed against the Virgin Mary's collar, as if he were about to tug on it and whisper the thief's name into her ear. On the other side was Saint Sebastian, arrows frozen mid-air aimed at his chest. The women said a prayer out loud, and Elsa, unpracticed in supplication, followed along. As their hands fell to their sides, one woman said that perhaps the saint in the icon had taken human form and slipped away.

Had the local suspects been cleared? She knew that Nico's name was sounding in their heads. "What about Anastasia?" Elsa acted as if she had just now thought of it. And she had. Anastasia Panusi, the widow with the wire-rimmed glasses, had lost her little girl a quarter of a century ago when the child had disappeared during the first round of Nazi burning. While the others were praising St. Christopher, Anastasia had gnashed her teeth and rubbed her worry beads 'til they turned to seed. Perhaps she had never forgiven the saint.

As the women lapped up the possibility of a new suspect, Elsa took a bite of a sesame cracker. She listened to bits of conversation from the hallway that led to the monastery chapel. "I didn't think it could be a *woman*?" Elsa collected the words and wrapped the sentences around her wrists. Her shift finally ending, she passed through the smell of incense in the chapel, the light from the yellowed stained-glass window darkening her skin. She caught two boys, adolescents, running half-naked through the monastery's halls, squirting water from plastic bottles at each other. "It's a *woman*," they cried. Their sandals flapped against their soles as they ran, their race ending at the front gate, amidst goats chewing on clumps of grass. Standing in the doorway, Elsa averted her eyes for a moment, then watched the water dripping from their brown skin and bangs. "You shouldn't waste that," she said as they tried to hide the bottles behind their backs.

❋ ❋ ❋

Back in the village, she circled around the taxi and kicked a tire. Inside the house, she opened the day's mail. Reading a notice, she cleared her throat, then walked down the hall and called out Nico's name. She heard the glide and flop of him taking a bath, then found him there, in the bathroom, in a tub of water reaching only halfway to the rim. His knees rested on opposite sides of the tub, his feet misshapen under the water's distortion. She couldn't remember the last time she had seen so much water under their own roof. On the tiled floor lay empty plastic bottles. She began to scold him, then knelt down and grabbed one of the empties.

"Where did you get all these?"

"I call it the 'smart man's plumbing.'" He shifted his bottom, sinking his shoulders under the water.

She held the letter in front of him. "Didn't you already serve in the army? Before we were married?" She could smell the soap on his skin.

He shook his head. "Get that away from me." He squeezed the loofah midair and watched the water rain on him.

She lifted her chin and spoke to a heaven in which she didn't quite believe.

"Who has time for the fucking army?" He looked up at her. "I'm going to the city," he said. "To drive that cab into its shallow grave." Beneath the water, he massaged one foot with the other. "And unload that icon to some blonde tourist."

"I told the women that Anastasia could have stolen it."

He stared at her, but it was his mouth that was most alive. It hung open. "Anastasia?"

They both knew that story, too. Anastasia's husband, upon discovering his child's body in pile of rubble, had her buried immediately, even before his wife had returned from her hiding place in the mountains. When she came back, she was told the news. She ordered her husband to dig up the grave and have one of her daughter's shoes, which smelled of rot and perfume, brought to her. As evidence. It was said her child's shoe, painted gold, hung in a corner of icons in her house.

"Throwing old women to the dogs. That's not like you," he said.

"You could at least thank me." She stood, dropped the letter, then grabbed her eyeliner from beside the sink.

"Close your eyes," she said.

He smiled and closed them. She noticed his long lashes as she began to write "bastard" on his forehead, but he flinched, then wiped at it with his palm.

"What are you doing?" He crashed his elbow against the side of the tub.

"Giving the devil his due."

She heard knocking at the door, then a voice—Nico's mother, Triada. Elsa dropped the eyeliner and made her way to the door.

"I'm coming."

"What the hell are you doing out there?" Nico yelled. Then, moments later, he emerged, in a robe, and stared at her, not blinking. Water dripped from his bangs.

She motioned to him. He grabbed the icon off the bed, then took a book off the shelf, a children's story of mermaids, one of the few things she had left from her childhood. He removed the dust cover, wrapped the icon inside it, and slipped it back on the shelf.

Elsa opened the door, and Triada stood before her, arms full of beets.

"My arms are breaking." Triada hurried to the counter and unloaded the beets.

Elsa blinked at Nico. Triada pulled open a drawer, grabbed a knife and began washing and slicing beets. Elsa filled a pot with water, thought about how she would save the water for soup. Triada scooped handfuls of sliced beets into the pot.

"Look at these happy beets in all this water."

"Let me finish dressing," Nico said as he left the room. Elsa and Triada traded guesses of how far the drought might spread, how nature ruled them in the end. Triada spoke of surviving other droughts in this pile of rocks they called a village. This was Nico's town, Elsa was reminded, not hers. Her stories lived elsewhere, in a burning village, her stolen mother, Elsa rising from the inside of an old tire in the middle of a war wearing a coat that was missing all its buttons.

Nico showed up at the dinner table with wet curls and smelling of shaving cream and cigarettes. They spoke about the junta, then switched to movie actors, Charlton Heston and Anthony Quinn. Elsa and Nico didn't mention how they were running out of money. Or how Elsa was still not pregnant, that she had no intention of becoming pregnant, an intentionally barren woman, the sign perhaps of a new era, but everything else had remained the same. The cucumber salad, diced precisely as it had been cut for generations, the *fasolatha*, cooked till the beans were soft as potatoes. They watched television for a while and lingered, the three of them, over coffee and biscotti. Then the silence came.

Triada folded and unfolded her napkin. "People are talking." She looked at Nico but couldn't manage to meet Elsa's eyes.

"They have always made up things about Nico because he is handsome," Elsa said.

"The whole town is a bunch of goddamn masturbators." Nico cleaned his teeth with his tongue.

Triada sighed and began to pick up the dishes, but Elsa stopped her and took the stack to the sink. Behind her, she heard Nico walking his mother to the door, something he never did, a sign of guilt or of the need to stretch his legs. Elsa wiped crumbs off the table but her eyes wandered to his feet as he paced from the bedroom side of the room to the kitchen.

"We can't wait any longer."

She lifted her head as Nico grabbed the icon off the shelf, took a paring knife, and jammed it into the right eye of St. Chrisopher. As he began to dig out the first sapphire, the saint's iris, she grabbed his arm and tried to push him to the floor, his elbow cracking against the wall. His watchband broke, and his watch fell to the floor. She grabbed the icon and began to run toward the back door. He grabbed her ankle. She tripped—the icon cracked on the tiled hallway—and caught herself on the doorframe. He rubbed his arm, then squatted and picked up the icon. "I'm not driving goddamn tourists to the Parthenon the rest of my life when I can sell these instead."

"And I'm supposed to hem wedding dresses till I go blind?"

"You're in this, too," he said.

"But somehow only you got a bath."

"They have more stories now than ever," he said. "Some of them think he turned human and walked away. The nuns love this shit. He turned human!"

"I'll be the one to go back to Athens," she said. "Watch me."

"Don't leave yet," he said. "I'll take you there myself on a motorcycle."

She got to her feet, ran out the door into the street, waited for a car to pass. There was nothing left to say to him, not after he'd jammed a knife in a saint's eye. A saint who carried Christ across the river, who had carried old women down the hallways of heaven, while Nico ferried blonde tourists across Athens and tried to sell them fake pebbles from the Parthenon. She crossed through a cloud of dust to the cafe on the other side of the street.

She bought an orange soda, walked out the back door with the cool bottle in her hand. She thought of the girls ten years younger than she was, girls born after the war and who went off to university and found civil engineers to marry in the city, young women who returned to the village only on holiday and found the festival of St. Mary quaint, marveled at the donkeys loaded with bags of pistachios. Mothers could walk into the future with their daughters. They could move in with them and coddle grandchildren while their husbands whistled their old age away at the cafenion. Elsa had never wanted children but now she wished she had one, a passage to the future, while Nico remained in his perpetual adolescence. She walked 'til the bottle in her hand was warm.

Back at her house, she opened the front door not knowing what crime was waiting her attention. The icon, its eyes hollowed out, lay on the floor.

"Bastard," she said. But he was gone. A plate with chunks of beets sat on the table. The dresses and tulle from the cab sat folded on a table in the corner. She scanned the room for the groom's tuxedo, but it was nowhere. "Lord." She looked out the front door and saw the glass shards on the street. The cab was gone.

She put down the bottle and sat on a chair, removed the watch wedged into her backside—another stolen trinket—and stared at the television screen till it turned to static. On the armrest was a clump of tulle and a tape measure. Her mind went to the fighting that would erupt when Nico returned, her fingernails on his throat. He was too lucky, as lazy men so often were, to wind up dead. He would return with jewels still in his shirt pocket, or with a roll of drachmas in his fist, money to burn, or his pockets filled with pebbles from the Parthenon, more myths to sell. Everything he was worth could fit in those pockets.

She picked up the icon, its eyes now sunken, the halo of gold erased to a shadow, chips of paint and wood falling to the floor. She slipped it into a plastic grocery bag. She went out into the moonlight. If they found the remains under her roof, she would have nothing to say. They would think of her as a willing passenger, along for Nico's ride. The shadow of a parked bicycle spilled across the street. With the bag close to her chest, like a hymnal, she walked past dark doorways and made her way to the other side of town, her eyes following the repeated whitewashed pattern on the sidewalk underfoot. She heard her own blood filtering through her body. Whatever fear had thrust her from her house out onto the streets as a girl running from war, separated forever from her real mother, was what now compelled her to make this trip: down the paved street, past the butcher's hovel, past the house with the large TV screen, second road on the right, to arrive here, at the yard with the deep cistern where men sometimes stole cupfuls of water. Beyond the yard Anastasia's stone house stood. Elsa's sandals crunched against the ground. She shook them off and felt the sudden silence, crept into the blackness, and stepped over shadows till she felt nothing but dirt beneath her feet. She removed the icon from the crinkly bag, just a simple square of wood in the dark. She kneeled and searched for stones, placed them inside the bag, then the icon. She made out the gray wall of the cistern. She leaned over, pushed up her sleeve, laid the icon bag in the water, the water filling the holes in the bag and cracks in the wood. She pushed the blind saint into the depths, her sleeves slipping into the water. As she turned and felt for the slit in the ground to lead her back to the street, she kneeled and looked for her sandals. She fingered the ground around her. Nothing.

She saw a flicker of light in the window. She stood and began walking, barefoot, her hands still wet when the door flew open. There, on the front stoop, as if stepping out of a fable, Anastasia stood in front of Elsa, hair in a bun. A dog lay beside her. Elsa quickened her pace.

"Wait."

Elsa stopped and faced the woman behind her. Anastasia wore a black dress and black hose stockings. Behind her, the white stone house glowed, wedges of light from the kitchen and hallway spilling onto the white adobe stairs. Even the old woman seemed to be lighted from within, her pale face and earlobes almost glowing.

"It's late." Anastasia's arms were folded.

"I was walking. It helps me sleep better." Elsa motioned to the yard. "I noticed that your cucumbers haven't dried up. I came closer to marvel."

"Are your keys still locked in that car?"

Elsa shook her head and curled her toes.

"Care for chamomile?"

Before she knew it, Elsa was inside the house, sipping tea, staring at the iconostasi in the corner that contained tales as fantastical as the myth surrounding Anastasia's own life—saints with mouths sewn shut and plants that shot out of the ground overnight. There was no shoe.

Insects flitted around the ceiling light in the kitchen, hitting against the glass. Elsa glanced at the newspaper on the table. Her eyes moved across the headlines—the Archbishop's visit, student protests. Anastasia scanned the length of Elsa's body and seemed to eye every vein of her exposed feet, every rib showing through her cotton dress.

"What are you eating," she asked. "Air?"

Elsa tried to laugh, glanced at the counter.

Anastasia slid a plate of cucumber chunks toward her. "Please get something besides grass and air in your body or you'll turn into a goat." This was always the custom, to pretend that a guest was too thin. Then it was time, after all, for Anastasia to walk slowly around the room and offer Elsa some katayifi, while Elsa rubbed her sleeve. Anastasia smelled of mothballs, of mouthwash, but it could not cover up the smell of skin and sweat. She grabbed Elsa's hand and squeezed. Elsa tightened her grip and felt the water she could not hide.

"So you finally got thirsty? Is that why you came?" Anastasia released Elsa's hand. "And you decided that my water was yours."

Anastasia thinned her eyes at her.

"I have water for everyone, but no water for thieves."

"I was taking a walk." Elsa stared at the tablecloth.

"Barefoot?"

Elsa swallowed.

"You hid a bucket somewhere and will be back for it. Ey?"

Elsa shook her head and got up, like a woman who suddenly remembered she had a chicken in the oven.

"I'll be watching you," Anastasia said.

"But I haven't—" Elsa attempted a nod, then slipped out of the house, the light from the front hallway spotlighting the front patio. She heard Anastasia walk out onto the front step, then she, Elsa, looked over at the cistern, felt her bare feet press into the earth. She heard, or thought she heard, the icon floating to the top, water bubbling around it. She heard Anastasia walking toward the well. Elsa resisted the urge to run, picked a weed, and pretended her mind was vacant. She sensed the sickle moon and the light from the entryway forcing her to walk into her own shadow. She scattered weeds like a flower girl at a wedding, preparing the way for the large white mystery behind her.

She heard a car barely moving beside her. She kept walking and then heard "Baby" and turned her head.

"I've been looking for you."

Inside the broken window she saw his half-smile, a smudge of eyeliner, perhaps a shadow, on his forehead. He wore the groom's tuxedo. The cab seemed out of place on a dark road in a village.

"You have no idea what you've done."

"If you say so." His brow crinkled, and he turned off the engine.

"You should have married him instead." He stared down at his tux.

"I don't have time for nonsense," she said.

When the engine started again, the sound, too, seemed out of place. His fingers drummed on the wheel.

"If we leave now, we'll be in Athens in time for—"

"See." She leaned over, drank him in for the last time, then opened the back door. "You forgot my sewing kit."

He lowered his head. "I'd take you to the moon if I could."

She got in the back seat, smelled the perfume and sweat of so many tourists, then felt shards of glass on the vinyl seat. He opened the glove box, lit a cigarette, and sat in silence.

"What would you say if I did my six months in the army? If I—" His voice broke.

She meditated and watched him lift his head, waited to see what story his eyes would tell next.

"I'm already gone," she said.

His black eyes finally in the mirror. "I know."

S-Curve

I stumble over the Greek alphabet
written in white, harvest,
rose chalk on the path between
the park and my office on campus.

Poor crooked spine,
the doctor said years ago.
*But you won't have problems
until you're 50.* After the pills,

I can revel and stretch
in those unreadable texts
made by children turned
loose here for art camp.

Outside my window, the maintenance
man, homeless once,
rides his bike to work, art
supplies in the basket,

a handlebar bell to announce
his hello. Against brick,
a tree's green above a
rickety air-conditioner. Wires, gutters,

windows that haven't been
opened for years. In these
last seven days of my forties,
I remember a friend saying,

like a feel-good chiropractic
poster, *It's good for your spine —
forgiveness.* He was fresh from
a retreat where former seminarians

smoked and cursed and hugged
women again, singing, he said, not
the holy hymns. Instead,
what they—*celebrants*

spread out in the merry world—
see now: the temples shaken, tables
overturned. They're a little bent
forward, still loved, and loving

the translated ruckus of gospel.

Kathryn Dunlevie, "Moses of East London,"
archival inkjet print on panel

Scrimshaw

So, I live in Pennsylvania, home of potato filling, cabbage slaw,
shoofly pie, apple butter, scrapple, red beet eggs, hog maw,
solid starchy stuff. But when I want to go wild, overdraw
my account, then I fly to Paris, change to a black lace bra,
matching panties. Stop at a bistro, eat oysters in the raw
with brown bread, unsalted butter, wine the color of pale straw,
then stroll down a leafy street, wander gardens I could draw
if I had talent. For a country girl, this is shock and awe:
even a folded napkin a work of art. I'm sure there are flaws,
but I can't see them. I prefer Pépé le Pew to Quick Draw McGraw,
Gérard Dépardieu to Brad Pitt, Isabelle Huppert to Kate Capshaw,
coq au vin to KFC, Bain de Soleil to Coppertone, scofflaw
that I am. Ray Charles said, *Tell your mama, tell your pa*
I'm gonna send you back to Arkansas,
but I don't want to go there, or to Utah or Omaha.
I want to stay in Paris for that *je ne sais quois.*

Kathryn Dunlevie, "Atelier Aimee," mixed media on panel

Meditation on Solitude and Simplicity

Pay here says the sign but I walk on by,
the street is filled with people and nobody

is paying. Men are assaulting the pavement
just outside Jamba Juice but I trust it will

be well in the end. My table is near the restrooms
which are occupied. The guy with the broom

has a beautiful purple shirt. The girl waiting
is biting her lip. She goes to the door

and hesitates. I think about being smart
vs. being useful. My pen is nearly dry

but I have another. It takes a lot of people
to provide this much solitude. Alfred

North Whitehead urges us to seek simplicity,
but not to trust it. Would I trade my life

for any of these others? No, no, yes, maybe.
Only if it came with a didgeridoo. Only if

it came with a nametag. Only if rides
on the free mall tram were included.

Only with blonde curls and almost
too young to be my daughter. Only

if I could have mine back any time.

Brain Science

Between Fairhope, Alabama, and Ocala, Florida,
I drove away from the sun until no lights
were left on the highway, just woods around the road, the
car, and washed-up bits of tires like seaweed
or the egg purses of eels. I felt like Dante's Dante:
midway upon the journey of life I found myself upon a forest dark
though I'm not as old, not midway, even as much as Florida
feels like hell, or caves under its own weight
into sinkholes that reach the slow-moving aquifer.
Minutes and miles into the darkness, a cell phone
running lower whenever I GPSed, and on
NPR a girl was hit by a semi-, already
deaf, now struck blind, and when her boyfriend
(whom her mother disliked—"I didn't like her look
when she looked at him") finally traced words
on her skin, Helen Keller-like, she said
"Oh how sweet. How nice of you" to his declaration
of love, the first words to reach her,
and hers to him spoken out loud, "I love you too.
Who are you?" Later, she told him,
Can you help, can you get me out? I'm trapped
behind this wall. In the car, alone,
I started to believe that she was there with me,
feeling the hands of strangers, hearing people
come in and out of her room, hallucinating
the lost senses. I was afraid that I was a figure
in the dream she couldn't wake up from.
When I called you from the hotel, you told me
you listened to the same Radiolab while painting the other day
(Florida NPR running reruns) and I heard the story again
with your voice as all the voices, and we're still
so far away from each other, I haven't seen you
since weeks before that conversation. I'm scared
that every dream will feel like being trapped inside a wall,
like my childhood fear of being buried alive,
and after I got home from Ocala I dreamt

I was locked in a prison with a man who was going to rape me,
at the beginning of the dream I was a reporter, maybe
that's how I figured out it was a dream, and when I told the man,
"I'm going to wake up," he took off his shirt, he said,
"Can you? can you really?"

Bob Evans, photograph

Eternal Life (The Running Poem)

(To be read *Accelerando*)

You and I running
        to catch the train for Warsaw
        is it always later than you think?
        pounding Krakow's cobbled streets
        we send up a flutter of birds, crash
        their pecking order as we
        strafe across the plaza, *clock 2:50,*
                train at 3:00,
        the desk clerk smiled, "They always leave on time . . ."

Ten minutes
        'til the tower bugler crows to flip the hour,
        tribute to an ancient warrior cut down
        by an arrow while he trumpeted a warning,
        (but) I can't stop to dwell on legends—fleeing
        now Hotel Elektor through an
        avalanche of twisted turns, maze of
        bone-bleach arched and artful architecture,

we are heavy
        in our winter coats this unexpected first
        warm day of spring *come home come home*
        a chorus to keep pace by, suitcase,
        shopping sacks fat with spoils of native glass
        bump hips bump thighs bang knees
        at every footfall—you beside me, but ahead

sweat pops
        through wool loops in your coat
        perspiration pools and burns our eyes,
        we shoot past cathedral gardeners,
        a dirge of rakes claws earth's dark skin,

there is panic
        at the pinch I'm in, wondering will my
        head burst first or heart *flap of coattails pulse*
        inside my ears imagine gardeners gardening
        open graves, turn back dank soil with that
        soft-same tawny scent—

stone,
                    handrail,
                                steps,

a baby's fist

                    shoots up from a parked pram, suspicious men
                    on benches turn away, they don't look up
                    as newsprint flutters in their hands,
                    do not look up to see us running
                    out of history, out of *time*, from salt mines
                    juxtaposed against this old and holy city—this

open market chokes

                    an entrance to the station, kiosks blur,
                    cabbage potatoes postcards spin, a bag
                    slips off my shoulder, I slow beneath a
                    clothesline clipped with t-shirt images
                    of Pope John in Small to X-tra Large

you call my name

                    to check I'm still in tow, *SEE BEAUTIFUL*
                    POLAND DOUBLE-TIME! we rush
                    the unsuspecting from behind—like cameras
                    strapped to a high-speed chase,
                    faceless backs who never saw us coming

push past

                    women *young, medium, old* parade of
                    Eastern Europe Costume—high-heeled shoes
                    sans stockings, thin dresses hammered into
                    kaleidoscopic swatches, Cold War Couture
                    *they never saw it coming—w*e take stairs

down two-by-two,

                    childhood asthma flares, heart wound
                    too tight thumps warning notes, the
                    bugler crowing, *Hey, your time is up!*

you yell

                    There is our train! and like movie stars
                    we bound the last car's step on cue—
                    a locomotive whistles,
                    hitches up its weight
                    and pulls away.

(Ritardando)

We slump against the train door facing trackward,
watch iron unfurl like ribbon, refracting light
from a frail and failing sun. You shake your topcoat
to the floor, then laugh as I remember how to breathe.
Somewhere
in the race between Elektor and the station,
IT passed before our eyes—the warning flash
of life's last snapshot, rumored panorama
that fans out for the dead? Or was it
                              life—chased
with an odd exhilaration, that having outrun
this small death, we are doomed to live forever.

(Fine)

Kathryn Dunlevie, "Platform Six," mixed media on panel

Cualacino

I lift my glass from the table.
A ring of water remains
on the counter, almost unbroken.
Italians call these rings
cualacino. My language
never made room for this word.

The last morning I saw you,
we lay perspiring, limbs
interlocked like frozen dancers
unfreezing. We
watched the room turn
gray and blue-gray. Later,
all that was left were sheets
pressed to the shape of our bodies.

A waitress stops, wipes away
the water ring, leaves
a silver streak glaring
up from the diner bar, and
I thirst for words:

white street the moon
makes on water;
dusted sun rays flicker
through tree leaves; a woman
waiting outside for her lover
to visit. I want

to name little sacred things that live
ghostlike after they're gone:
mangata, komorebi, hiðrutsi,

words we can't use
during phone calls, in goodbyes,
when paying for lunch,
when loving. Our tongues won't shape

right, our vocal chords won't stretch
the correct pitch.

Together for the last time,
mouths eternally shut,
I dressed at the foot of the bed,
you dressed by the door.

Eleanor Leonne Bennett, photograph

Snow White

They said, "We could not bury her in the dark ground,"
and they had a transparent coffin of glass made,
so that she could be seen from all sides,
and they laid her in it.

When I was dead, I
could hear them weeping, little men
crying because I slept, slept so soundly
they dared not move my cold body
from where I lay flat and still
as a snake before it peels.

I could taste the tart on my tongue,
where the meat of the flushed apple met
my mouth, melted right into my lips
and down my throat like honey and wax,
sweet and warm before it hardened
like the candle after the flame,
and my breath stopped.

I want to lie in the ground,
to slip from my skin, to breathe
the same earth into my lungs
that every man tastes in living and
dying. I want to feel the dirt between my fingers
like a plow. I want to grow wheat from my stomach,
a field of gold and sweat and muscle.

But I am a shell inside a paperweight,
the snow inside a globe
that they watch and watch,
and never think that maybe, just
maybe, they should let me fall.

The Unrhymables

Orange

   "Oranges poranges—who said there ain't no rhyme for oranges?" My sister and I loved this song from H.R. Pufnstuf, a show about—well, who can say? On Saturday mornings, we'd watch it with my father who sang the show's theme song, "H.R. Pufnstuf, who's your friend when things get rough?" "Stuff" and "rough," real words, rhymed perfectly. Some critics now think that the friendly dragon Pufnstuf (along with *Scooby-Doo*'s Shaggy) was a stoner. I have to admit he did say, "Whoa dude!" a lot. Making up words to rhyme with oranges—ploranges, foranges, choranges—gave my sister and me hours of pleasure, and sometimes my dad would join in, asking, "What about broranges?"

   Oranges are the state fruit of Florida, the place I live now, though I seldom see them in supermarkets. I read that most of the good oranges grown here are sent north. When I lived in New York, I'd buy oranges at the Korean grocer and then rub the pith onto my teeth to make them whiter, and it worked. Though ghosts are usually depicted as white, *Scooby-Doo's* 10,000 Volt Ghost was orange. Shaggy and his friends figured out why. The ghost wasn't a former workman killed by a power surge but a live person in an orange rubber suit hired to scare away townspeople. Casey Kasem, who was the voice of Shaggy, insists his character was a wholesome guy. Sid and Marty Kroft, the creators of *H.R. Pufnstuf*, maintain they used no intentional drug references.

   Why do oranges seem less symbolically fraught than apples? There are exceptions, of course. Jeanette Winterson's *Oranges Are Not the Only Fruit* aligns oranges with repression, heterosexuality, the status quo. And some see the death of Jesus in blood oranges, popular in Sicily, which leads me to the movie *The Godfather* and all those oranges rolling across the street as Don Corleone gets shot. *The Godfather's* set designer Dean Tavoularis said that the oranges were used to contrast against the dark, somber sets. Nothing about Jesus or sacrifice. My father died right before Thanksgiving, and there aren't any words that rhyme with Normand. " Suze Orman?" I ventured a near rhyme, even though her surname has no "d." My sister and I tried to brighten up the gray Rhode Island skies above the cemetery with bouquets of orange zinnias and daylilies.

Angst

Let's talk about angst. Let's talk about a word straining at its vest, too bulky to be the single syllable it is: a word in identity crisis. Let's talk about adjectives that cozy up to angst in the library, where understandably angst spends a lot of its time. Mostly a loner, angst has been spotted with *teen*—a girl with gap teeth who takes long pauses in the middle of her sentences, pauses that seem in fact to accentuate those gaps she chose over braces—and *existential*—a bad-boy type who saves his cigarette butts to keep an accurate record of the number of minutes he is shaving off his life. (Eight minutes per cigarette means 160 minutes per pack means 1600 minutes per carton . . .) He is also ideologically committed to stunting his growth.

Let's talk about angst—or *ahhhhngst*, as my German friend says. In her version, I hear the sound I make when the doctor depresses my tongue. Angsty people have been known to lose their appetites, as if the tongue were truly depressed and couldn't muster the verve required for lifting or tasting food. But to be in angst isn't the same as being depressed. It isn't even exactly Kafkaesque, though I'd wager Gregor Samsa might claim them both—the angst at finding himself transformed giving way to the depression that drives him from home. His problems are well beyond semantic by the end.

Let's take it a shade lighter, if we can. Let's talk about the color of angst, which to my synesthetic mind is burnt-orange and smoldering like Velma's turtleneck sweater. Let's talk about angst and Velma Dinkley from *Scooby-Doo*, who hid hers well behind a magnifying lens and a hokey catch phrase. (*Jinkies!*) Let's talk about angst and the problem of the wobbly third wheel. Shaggy has Scooby. Fred has Daphne. When they split up, Velma is always somebody's tag-along.

Did you know the name Velma derives from Wilhelmina? Did you know it comes from the Greek for "strong-willed warrior"? Most popular in the United States in 1950, the name is favored by those who also like Penelope and Ophelia—women who waited for men, raveling, and women who stopped waiting for men.

When I told my father I liked Velma best, he patted my head. "Well, she does solve the mysteries," he said, "but don't you see how Daphne is the happier girl?"

Breadth

"Measure his woe the length and breadth of mine," says Leonato in *Much Ado About Nothing.* Even though the play is considered one of Shakespeare's great comedies, I think Leonato had a point. How can you comfort someone whose sadness is beyond what you comprehend? How can you say, "Hang in there!" without seeing that poster of a cartoon kitty, front paws clutching a pull-up bar? How can you hold the true breadth of another's pain?

Breadth contains both bread and breath. Hatred and heart. Earth and herb. Heat and head. Herd and bather. Breadth contains my grandmother Bertha who died when I was thirteen, during my first period. Breadth contains bra, my new terrifying breasts. Breadth contains brat, my guilt for not visiting Bertha as much as I should have that last year. Breadth contains bard, my adolescent poems locked in a diary.

I didn't have the breadth of experience to truly comfort my mother who had just lost her mother. My grandmother had lost her own mother when she was just thirteen because my great-grandmother had asthma like I do now. My grandmother's mother slept in a chair so she wouldn't choke. The family boiled eucalyptus for her, as there were no inhalers back then. Since her own mother was gone by the time my grandmother's first period came, there was no one around to explain the bleeding. She ran into a barn and lay with the sheep, sure then that she was dying. She'd lived all these extra years.

My mother curled into me. She was warm and heaving. I was almost as tall as she. My hips almost the breadth of hers.

In the restroom of the funeral parlor was a full-length mirror on the inside door and another full-length mirror on the wall directly behind it. As I checked my lip gloss and smoothed the skirt my grandmother Bertha had sewn for me just a few weeks before, I caught the reflection of my mother behind me and there, in the mirror behind us, we stretched into infinity—my mother, then me. My mother, then me. My mother, then me. "Let's go," she said, touching my shoulder. I blinked, unable to articulate what I was seeing—ghosts, babies. Mother and daughter in bodies, in between.

We walked to my grandmother's coffin. My mother knelt on the red velvet, then I squeezed in beside her.

Depth

My mother lost her mother the week I turned thirteen, the same day in fact that I lost the Miss Pre-Teen America Pageant. I had spent all summer preparing my speech, my sonatina, my runway turn and look. My grandmother had spent all summer preparing for the end. Sometimes I walked with a book on my head beside her hospital bed—what my mother promised would improve my posture: "Stop slouching! There's nothing wrong with being tall!"

And my grandmother, whose lush gray curls had thinned to wisps of white, pointed at me: "Who does she think she is?"

"That's *Julie*, Mama. That's your *granddaughter*, Julie. You have *four* granddaughters . . . ."

"I know!" she snapped, her IV lines shaking like so many tangled ghosts. "But Julie's no beauty queen. *Blythe* is the beauty queen."

Of course my grandmother was right. My mother blamed her outbursts on the drugs, but she had never been kind in real life—only blunt, which seemed to me now a better way of being honest. Maybe I could learn to love her after all.

Was I out of my depth when I discovered my mother was no longer home to monitor meals? My father ate with the television on. He helped himself to second helpings, assumed I did the same. Was I out of my depth when I learned to favor watermelon over bread, cantaloupe over chocolate, honeydew over every other food? They taught us at Lenten service that it meant nothing to give up something you didn't love. Surely Jesus had savored his life on earth—all those loaves and fishes, to say nothing of that sweet red wine. If he could lay down his life for us, what could we relinquish from our own?

But it wasn't Lent; it was August. My parents had paid someone to bulldoze our green-grass yard and carve out a swimming pool shaped like a kidney bean. I was so hungry by then everything resembled food. Was I out of my depth when I couldn't stop counting the laps anymore? When I lost control of my limbs and felt the water creeping into my lungs? My father stood on the deck and called down, "How 'bout some popcorn and a movie, Smidge?" I saw him glassy above the water before I began to sink. The deep end was only nine feet, but my father dove in and saved me.

Purple

My sixth-grade teacher "Flat-As-A-Board" Hoard was the first teacher I had who was a Ms. She was lanky and wore a purple turtleneck under her overalls, the bib of which would flap this way and that. My guess is that Ms. Hoard was naturally thin, as she kept a jar of purple jellybeans right on top of her desk. She explained to us the tenets of feminism and how feminism, like a flag or a sports team, even had colors—purple, white, and gold, which symbolized loyalty, purity, and hope. She convinced us all—boys and girls alike—that we were at the crux of an amazing movement. We were part of the first class to have co-ed recess. The ERA was just being introduced to Congress. Though I didn't have any purple shirts, I bought purple shoelaces for my sneakers.

When Ms. Hoard found out about her nickname, she didn't get angry. Instead she told our class that we should love our bodies as they were, accept the miracle of them. My smile contained a wince as I was already quite aware of my pudginess. My grandmother sewed most of my outfits because back then clothing from stores cost too much. But, every once in a while, when I could choose something as a gift, I had to find it in the "chubette" pages of the Sears catalogue. Like Ms. Hoard, my grandmother must have accepted my body—she once let me eat a whole sleeve of her Walkers shortbread cookies.

My grandmother was Scottish and knew some Gaelic words and dialect. If in sixth grade I'd have known who Robert Burns was, I'd have asked her to help me make sense of his poem "Epistle to Mrs. Scott," the last stanza of which contains these lines:

> I'd be mair vauntie o' my hap,
> Douce hingin owre my curple,
> Than ony ermine ever lap,
> Or proud imperial purple . . .

"Curple" sounds suspiciously like "poranges" to me, but apparently it means the rump of a horse! I guess Burns might be saying he's as proud of the modest clothes he wears over his bottom as a king wearing royal pants. I'm not sure if that's it exactly, but I think Ms. Hoard would have applauded Robert Burns' individualism (he's probably the only poet to ever use the word "curple"), his appreciation of his attire, his station in life, and his rear.

Gulf

In simplest terms, gulf is a water word—a deep sea inlet surrounded by land with a narrow channel for passing in or out. Like middle school, a gulf is a likely place to drown.

When I skipped sixth grade, I learned about another gulf— wider than a gap, more brutal than a fissure. Let's call it the abyss between theory and practice, the void between ideal and real: to be the youngest student in the class, to be the flattest student in the class, and everyone watching, taking note, hell-bent on my burgeoning. Nancy Twedt approached me with a grin, then pressed her index fingers hard against my new breasts, shouting, "Ding dong!" at the top of her lungs. Sarah Hemme ran her hand up the back of my legs before gym. "Porcupine!" she screeched. "Someone should get this girl a razor for her birthday." Danica Wetzel put out a cigarette on a teacher's car. "Let's cut to the chase, Curlicue—do you even use tampons or what?"

I didn't. I hadn't yet begun to bleed. But I stopped at the 7-Eleven after school and spent two weeks' allowance on a blue box with a dubious diagram inside.

So a woman's body was a gulf, too, I realized. It scared me to think of the places I couldn't see or reach, but I dreaded mirrors more than my own ignorance. An older girl from the high school said: "You've only got two choices: either pop that cherry yourself or wait for the wrong boy to do it for you."

This was years before I saw *Carrie*, Sissy Spacek's stricken face in the shower as a chorus of girls shouted, "Plug it up! Plug it up!," pelting her with tampons and pads. This was years before my boyfriend said, "This won't hurt, I promise, because I love you." Before the gynecologist asked, the furrow deepening between her brows: "Were you ever heterosexual?" Before I learned that some poems have pauses called *caesuras* in the middle of the line—that necessary space for silence, reappraisal. Before I read Suzanne Paola's "Red Girl" and discovered language was a rescue raft sent out into the gulf where I was flailing:

To turn woman is to turn
body:
what you are is who's touched you,
where they've touched—

When she kissed me, my eyes fluttered, then closed. An honest desire engulfed me at last.

Month

I used my knuckles to figure out which months had thirty-one days and was glad when I went from one hand to the other for July and August, those two long months of summer. I felt ripped off on days when I sunned myself, pretending that I was uninterested in the pool, the bulky wet Kotex between my legs. I feared tampons as a teenager and never truly got the hang of them. I wore a pad on the day I was married because my period had been late so I was still dribbling as I said, "I do." I had tried hard to plan for a menses-free honeymoon, but periods weren't always as predictable as the moon, which doesn't really fall that neatly into calendar months even though "moon" and "month" are cognates, from the Latin for *cognatus* (blood relative.) I made my first communion in Woonsocket, Rhode Island, at Precious Blood Church — also known by its French name, *L'Eglise du Precieux Sang*. In French, moon and month — *lune* and *mois* — don't seem quite as close.

The Catholic Church devotes the month of July to Precious Blood, the sacrament brought through Jesus' pierced side at Calvary. But by the time I was old enough to question the logic, I was devoting the month of July to tanning. Rather than make my confirmation, I did my astrology chart, my sun sign and moon sign both in Gemini. At least four of me wrestled inside my brain. No wonder I was moody and quixotic, regardless of what time of the month it was.

When my friends and I found the stack of *Playboys* in the woods behind our street, we gawked at each Playmate of the Month. Transfixed, we were speechless before Miss April's skin that looked as though it had been shellacked. She stood nude, totally unembarrassed, in some kind of tiki hut. (Turn-ons: Tall guys. Men with senses of humor. Turn-offs: Bad hygiene. Rain.) Miss November leaned against a pinball machine, wearing only snakeskin boots. Miss February posed naked except for a scarf and bent toward the curling handles of a white ten-speed bike. None of the scenarios made any sense. None of these women wore a pad or had the telltale sign of a tampon string.

In a few months, construction started. Bulldozers took down the trees, ripped through all those magazines, and a new housing development sprouted.

Mulct

There are some words we never say aloud. *Mulct* is one of them. It sticks in the throat like glue. It tastes worse than oatmeal without the raisins and brown sugar. But we know about mulcts, don't we? I'd wager every mother's daughter does.

In high school, we had to pay for pads and tampons if we forgot our own, if we were caught off guard in the lunch line or on our way to mass. Sister Dorothy, the school nurse, would dispense Tylenol for a headache, Band-Aids for a cut, but feminine hygiene required a quarter, a pause before the glossy white box in the bathroom with *KOTEX* scripted in silver.

"It isn't fair," I whined. "I wanted to buy chocolate milk with that money."

"I'm surprised you're surprised," my mother said, as if it were a tacit understanding. "Women always earn less but pay more."

In a few years, I would work for a university that promised not to profit from women's bodies. Bathrooms were stocked with the same folded packets, the same paper sheaths, but all the doors to the glossy white boxes were open. *Take what you need, ladies. They're free.* I was young, I was broke, I was indignant. I didn't like the world I'd grown into, where men still made crude remarks about women "on the rag," women "riding the cotton pony." All the mulcts weren't fiscal, you see. Some taxes were attached to my sex that I could never file or pay.

And so I filled a bag with a dozen pads, thirty or forty tampons. I was going to take them all back, reclaim my power through pseudo-thievery. I would never shell out money again for the ignominy of a "sanitary napkin." As I trudged toward Forbes Avenue, I noticed people peering at me from under their hats. A few less subtle folks were laughing. Then, a student rolled past on a wobbly bike: "I think you have a hole in your purse," she murmured.

I did what they say you should never do, stopping then to look back. The pads formed a trail like fallen leaves, the tampons like twigs marking my boot-prints against the packed snow. Was I Gretel after all—a girl majoring in consequence, primed for retracing her steps? I let the bag fall from my shoulder. I summoned my breath. I strode on to the bus stop, numb.

Silver

I'd once hoped to make it to a silver anniversary, twenty-five years with the same person, our silver hair finally devoid of its childhood colors, our forks and knives in a drawer just so. My husband convinced me that our sterling tea set, an assortment of heavy platters, ladles, and serving spoons, would be enough to get us through retirement. His parents gave us the heirlooms when they moved to a smaller apartment, and we shipped them to our place in Florida and even hid them in a locked closet when we went on vacation. During the divorce, I forgot all about the silver. When my ex came to pick up his stuff, he forgot, too. It wasn't until a few months later, when I was totally broke from our settlement, that I remembered I might be rich! I unlocked the closet and hugged each bowl.

I drove to an antiques dealer, ready to cash in. *Maybe I'd give my husband half,* I told myself, *maybe I wouldn't.* My trunk was brimming. I was brimming. I took in just the teapot ready to bargain, ready to say there was more where this silver came from.

I put my sunglasses atop my head and walked into the dark world of cuckoo clocks, maroon Oriental rugs, and Victorian settees.

It was hot and dusty. I sneezed and adjusted my eyes before spotting a silver-haired man behind a glass case full of gold rings and watches. He was shuffling receipts.

"May I help you?" he asked.

I held out the teapot, ready to be a wealthy divorcée. I wondered if I'd have to report this windfall on my taxes, if my ex would somehow find out and sue me. Maybe I should give him his share even though he was mean.

"This is silver-plated," the man said.

I smiled as though that was a good thing.

"Not interested." The man went back to his paperwork.

When I pressed him, he explained the process of getting the thin layer of silver off the pot was more expensive than what the silver was worth.

"I have more in my trunk," I said, trying to be optimistic. "Maybe that stuff's sterling?"

The silver-haired man reluctantly followed me to my Honda to tell me things were once again not what I'd hoped. When I cried he gave me a business card for a pawnshop on State Road.

Ninth

On my ninth birthday, I waltzed into the kitchen and announced, "Today I'm almost a woman!"

There I stood, halfway between footie pajamas and button-fly jeans, while my parents appraised me like a panel of judges. "Emphasis on the *almost*," my mother said, returned to stirring her tea.

Ninth the Not-Quite, I came to see. Not quite a decade or a double digit. Ninth the Nearly, the Honorable Mention, the silver-plated numerical mark trying to pass for something of higher value.

My friend Joy went to a feel-good school where every student always won a prize. She started aiming for ninth place because she loved the lavender ribbon. "Aren't you supposed to always do your best?" I said.

"I don't like blue as well as purple," she replied.

In Bible school, we memorized the Ten Commandments, which were arranged in order from greater to lesser crimes. *But how was cursing or sassing your parents worse than murdering someone?* I asked, aghast. And what about this Ninth Commandment, "Thou shalt not covet thy neighbor's house"? Such a simpler rule than the next one: "Thou shalt not covet thy neighbor's wife [. . .] or anything that belongs to thy neighbor." *It was worse somehow to covet his dwelling place than all the contents therein?*

The teacher gave me a lollipop and patted my head, suggested I take an early recess.

The ninth element on the periodic table is fluorine, easily forgotten and easily misspelled (the o and u reversed), though it is the most electronegative and reactive of all.

The ninth state admitted to the union was New Hampshire, whose motto is a charged imperative: *Live free or die.*

For a ninth anniversary, married couples should consider gifts of pottery or willow. Leather is a modern-day addition to the list, a twist on the old tradition.

Right now the Ninth Circuit Court of Appeals is considering the constitutionality of state-level bans on same-sex marriage. For many years, I have not coveted my neighbor's wife, but my neighbor's right to marry the woman he loves. Isn't *till death us do part* the spousal equivalent of *live free or die*? I have worn the lavender ribbon of domestic partnership, some pale version of better than nothing when nothing but equal will do.

"But you have to admit—it's almost as good as being married," the naysayer said.

I vaporized to fluorine right before her eyes.

Twelfth

The Twelfth Amendment to the United States Constitution changed the way we vote. Before 1804, the person with the most votes was president, while the person who came in second was vice president. I'm saying person—but, let's face it, I mean white man. All the voters were white men as well. In 1796, John Adams had the most votes, while Thomas Pinckney, the man he wanted for vice president, came in third. So Thomas Jefferson, Adams' rival with many opposing views on policy, became second in command.

Jefferson said of Adams that he "sometimes decided things against his counsel by dashing and trampling his wig on the floor." When Adams ran against Jefferson the second time he smeared him—because Jefferson supported the French Revolution, we could expect guillotines in America if he were elected.

Now presidential hopefuls, backed by corporations, run in likeminded pairs, their destiny decided by the Electoral College. Each sound bite is calculated, "talking points" ad nauseam.

It's hard to be nostalgic for a time of bondage for most people, and yet, what I wouldn't give to see a frustrated president stomp on his or her wig! Or political opponents suddenly president and vice-president, bickering like *The Odd Couple*.

What I wouldn't give to go back to the Christmas my father and all the uncles argued about Tricky Dick as they smoked cigars in the garage. One cousin was proud he threw an egg at Nixon's car. Another cousin was in Vietnam. If I could do it again, I would have left the world of my mother and the aunts who sang the round, "On the twelfth day of Christmas my true love sent to me: twelve Drummers Drumming . . . ." I would have sided with my father and said, "Thou shalt not kill!" to shame my religious pro-war uncle. I would have practiced my budding debate skills. When encountering Sharon Olds's "On Reading a Newspaper for the First Time as an Adult," I remember how watching the 11 o'clock news gave me nightmares. So I withdrew, the folly of politics making me feel powerless and exhausted. I was not truly "a reader of the earth's gossip."

Thomas Jefferson and John Adams reconciled after their political careers were done, and these signers of the Declaration of Independence became avid correspondents. On July 4, 1826, Thomas Jefferson and John Adams died within five hours of each other.

Wolf

If I could do it again, I would choose the Wolf instead of the hand-wringing mother. I would revel in the role of anti-hero at last, pushing the limits of fang and fur.

Mandie Salazar, the girl I loved, had been cast as Little Red Riding Hood. Mrs. Miller, the teacher I loved, said I needed to learn how to be good. "Sometimes being good means sharing the stage, even when you think you'd make a better star."

If I could do it again, I would seduce Red in the painted wood rather than send her out the door with an empty picnic basket. I would say, "Stray with me!" and take her smooth hand in my costumed paw. As her mother, I could only shout from the threshold: "Stay on the path! Stick to the straight and narrow!"

Then, I would sail ahead to graduate school, to the Cinema and Desire class, to Neil Jordan's *Company of Wolves*. In this story, victim and villain are brilliantly merged. Rosaleen, as proxy for Riding Hood, transforms into a wolf herself. She flees to the wilderness with her huntsman-wolf, members of a growing pack.

Who said her cape should be red anyway? Why not orange or purple or silver even, as Dorothy's original shoes? Some scholars suggest red represents the first menses, our young pilgrim's month of initiation into the angst of womanhood. Some scholars suggest our pilgrim was in her ninth year; others insist it was her twelfth. Regardless: who said Red was ready to strike out on her own? There was the breadth of the forest to consider, the depth of the river, the great gulf between imagination and experience on the lonely road to Grandmother's house.

If I could do it again, I would read Allen Tate's "The Wolves" before I read the tale of Riding Hood and long before I appeared in the play:

> I have brooded on angels and archfiends
> But no man has ever sat where the next room's
> Crowded with wolves [...]

I think every girl has. I think every girl has been Red with wonder and fury and terror at the Wolf beyond her, and the Wolf within. Every girl has been charged a mulct for passing through those woods. But not every girl has had the map of a poem to guide her. Not every girl has read a poem that doesn't rhyme.

Amanda Gannon, "Lonely Stars Cry," ink on paper

The Witch Introduces the Children

I hear little voices singing
through these woods, high voices lilting

over lullabies to make them feel
safe. *Hansel, here is the song our mother*

sang to us. Hear how her lungs fill with air
beneath her small chest. *Make us*

a bed beside that tree and I will sing
us both to sleep. See how the boy's

quick hands gather a pile of dry leaves
for his sister's head. As darkness

unrolls, they huddle together.
Song deserts them. Breath after

breath they whisper: *no such thing,*
no such thing, no such thing

The Witch Implicates the Children

All this past year, in your father's house, there has been hunger,
your small bellies churning empty through the night,
limbs slim and stunted.

Oh, in the first light there might be stale black bread,
but no gruel to soak it in. The last of your milk teeth crack
clean through, little stones you spit into your palms.

And still, beneath the strings of your dead mother's apron,
that woman's belly swells. At supper, she stirs fat in her own bowl,
greases her bones, eyes each scrap your father passes you.

Who would believe that you didn't desire this? That you didn't walk here
on your own unsteady feet? This house rises from the forest
like a fairy dream, all gingerbread

and candy suckets. What more could you have wanted?
I built it just for you.

The Witch Imagines a Fairy Tale in which the Girl Saves Herself

And what happens to the girl if there is no
strong woodsman?
Or if she is not pretty?
                    Or kind?   Or good?
What happens to the girl
                    if she is more
                                    like the wolf?

What has the girl ever been but something to be taken?
Do you think she does not know this?

Look how the silver light   catches
            the lines of her body.

She is a snare set in the forest.
                    She is ready to spring.

Eleanor Leonne Bennett, photograph

Portrait

Let's run through it again.
Complexion—geisha white.

Cheeks—deep pink (too deep).
Hands—closed petals in her lap.

The young lady is sitting in
. . . call it an elm.

Two blood-red horses share her limb.
They're screamingly small and seem to be blind.

Nothing will come of this, she muttered in Finnish.
Don't worry, he whispered, *apart from the pink*

all is utterly perfect. She looked aside.
The sky wilted for an instant.

Come, my dear, we're nearly there.
She lifted her eyes. The look was ancient.

It pierced the canvas and went on forever.

Process

(after de Kooning)

1.

Each unlikely, almost
manic pink
figures stripped and ripped   —a slip
of turquoise green
redressed then printed
over

drip traced charcoal twisted;
wet gobs and stabbed
chalk-stubs, caulked
fast, this fisted

with a palette knife
playpen of
paint.

2.

Art is charisma, my father-in-law says,
mid-stair at MOMA, a chopper overhead.
Our wives ditch to see Diego Rivera.
Francis Bacon beckons. Oils thicken
in canvas nests with blue bruises
and teeth in its neck.

To Dust

I can think of no one to set up
with your cousin. No friend or enemy
springs to mind. Not Mrs. Watkins
booked solid with grandchildren, or Coach Hector
in his red turtleneck and a division title
still on the line. Forgive me
my incompetence, this chronic desire
to wipe you clean. My fourth-grade crush
shushed at her recital. Shy Uncle Simon
stuck in your throat. I want to dig
my finger in there and get him. Let him rest
on my shoulder the whole ride home.

Shoshana Kertesz, photograph

Cicada

When what we love returns to us, expect it
to enter through the ear, as noise made
by some unexpected source, perhaps a body
foreign to our own. Tonight, a mango moon
swims at the edge of a sky swathed
in factory smoke and dust from roads.
Trilling from the campos filters through the open window
of a bedroom, harsh to the ear of a man
who, tossing and turning in his sleep, remembers mountains
and a girl whose face he sees only in dreams. This is the way it is
on earth—the particulate of the day settles in at night,
staining the sheets. A steady rasp from the bushes gives rise
to memory. Clarity comes briefly. Then the dark gives way
to tin dawns over corrugated roofs. Fires are stoked in factories.
Traffic noise begins.

Silent Mail

After a drouth, news of you comes to me
by word of mouth. In the house where we lived,
everything has been tidied and packed away: envelopes full of stammer
and spilt milk, chapped avowals—what does it matter now?
I've forgotten the gesture of the wrist, the words I rehearsed
again and again before the mirror, what I said
to make our goodbyes stick.

From the collection of the Senior Advisory Editor, photograph

Sea

We buried Mihalis today, we buried him
at noon, in the heat of August
in the early afternoon
with his mother wailing over the casket,
her eyes bruised from so much crying.
It was a record temperature afternoon
and people came in black,
some quiet, despite their raw looks.
We could not believe we were burying Mihalis,
the tall, statuesque man who strode
so firmly through his life,
who walked into the nearby hills
to take in the span of the city,
his laugh raucous and wide,
a laugh that pulled you out
of your own life to feel something even larger
than him, and solid, like his hands
that could clasp you fully
when he wrapped them around you,
or held your face within the world of his palms.
You could let go with Mihalis,
you could let yourself fall and know
he would gather you up.
For him to die suddenly
is as if the sea you expect to see
in its azure and sapphire depths
is suddenly not there, as if after walking many long hours
in the heat to reach its waves, expecting
the weight of your exhausted body
will be lifted in that satin embrace,
like the scent of jasmine in rain
. . . all that keeps you walking in your despair
sure of that sheer blue . . .
after all the sun, after your desperate exhaustion
you find you're mistaken,
the road you're on is much longer
and drier and more yellow,
and there's not even a glimpse of the sea, only earth
everywhere, and Mihalis gone.

Ghazals

زین گلستان درس دیدارِ که می خوانیم ما
اینقدر آینه نتوان شد که حیرانیم ما
عالمی را وحشتِ ما چون سحر آوازه کرد
چین فروشی دامانِ صحرای امکانیم ما
غیر عریانی لباسی نیست تا پوشد کسی
از خجالت چون صدا در خویش پنها نیم ما
هر نفس باید عبث رسوای خود بینی شدن
تا نمی پوشیم چشم از خویش عریانیم ما
در تغافل خانهٔ ابروی او چین می کشیم
عمرها شد نقشبند طاقِ نسیانیم ما

This garden preaches one message:
its mirror cannot reflect my awe. Magically,
my fear circumferences the world.
Seller of used goods, I inhabit the edge of the desert's possibility.
Since there are no clothes to wear, I clothe myself in nakedness.
I conceal myself from shameful sounds.
Until I dress my eyes in my nakedness, until,
in the house of forgetfulness, I fold my brow,
my every breath will be in vain. When I am gone,
my life will meld with the inscriptions on the mosque's dome.

س آشفته می دارد چو گل جمعیّتِ ما را
پریشان می نویسد کلک موج احوال دریا را
درین وادی   که می باید گذشت از هرچه پیش آید
خوش آن رهرو که در دامانِ دی پیچید فردا را
به این فرصت مشو شیرازه بند نسخهٔ هستی
سحر هم در عدم خواهد فراهم کرد اجزا را
به آگاهی چه امکان است گرد جمع خود داری
که با هر موج می باید گذشت از هیچ دریا را
چرا مجنونِ ما را پریشانی وطن نبود
که از چشمِ غزالان خانه بر دوش است صحرا را

Breathing tenses on our peaceful bouquets.
The waves inscribe the sea's stages nervously.
In this desert that is our destiny, we must face what we pass.
Blessed is the passerby who makes tomorrows of yesterdays.
Don't let the book's binding crumble while the dawn
illumines the fragments of our nothingness.
Who is served by what we see? Who profits
when the waves that crash do not reach the sea?
Why did the crazed Majnun not long for his homeland?
In the eyes of his poems, he carried his home through the desert on his body.

تاب زلفت سایه آویزد به طرف آفتاب
خطِ مشکینت شکست آرد به حرف آفتاب
دیده در ادراک آغوش خیالت عاجز است
ذرّه کی یابد کنار بحر ژرفِ آفتاب
ظلمتِ ما را فروغ نور وحدت جاذب است
سایه آخر می رود از خود به طرف آفتاب
بس که اقبالِ جنونِ ما بلند افتاده است
می توان عریانی ما کرد صرفِ آفتاب
در عرق عاجازِ حسنِ او تماشا کردنی است
شبنم گل می چکد آنجا ز طرفِ آفتاب
هر کجا با مهرِ رخسارِ تو لاف حسن زد
هم ز پرتو بر زمینَ افتاد حرف آفتاب
ما عدم سرمایگان را لاف هستی نادر است
ذرّه حیران است در وضع شگرفِ آفتاب
جانفشانیها ست بیدل در تماشای رخش
چون سحر کن نقدِ عمرِ خویش صرفِ آفتاب

Your hair shines from the sun's shadow.
Your musk lines break in the sun's letters.
Imagination founders when overcome by love.
The pearl on the edge of the sea is a deep sun.
To me, your oppression is freedom from the light.
The last shadow passes from itself to the sun.
Even after our wild fortune has fallen low,
the sun still shines on our nakedness.
Sinking miraculously, its light frolics beautifully.
The flower's dew cuts through the sun.
Everywhere, your face is overwhelmed
by its beauty as its rays strike the earth.
It is a rare gift to boast of nothingness.
The pearl of astonishment blooms beneath the sun,
selling the soul while gliding over your face. Bidel,
like the dawn, make your movement through life a turn to the sun.

Translated from the Persian by Rebecca Gould

Billets Doux

The first was returned unanswered.
How can you answer a blank page?
Later he said
you opened it didn't you?

The second one had two pages,
four words:
Don't answer
this yet

which for some reason made me
swallow a sob. I thought of time
passing, of Du Fu wanting the
Anshan rebellion to end.

I wanted to go home again.
As if there'd been an act
of nature and I walked a city
in flames. Everything startled me.

The third was a whole page
erased. The pencil imprint
was deep, I think from a Blackhawk
three. I use a number one,

rub sideways across the paper
with my fingertip over the point.
Not too heavy, not too light.
When the words emerge

even the paper
gets goose bumps.

Billet Doux

You're a bony, rangy old thing
asking for love

You go to your desk
and worry a line, worry a line

Flat-footed, crick in your neck
What a rickety mess

Never think for a second
I don't want you

If You Can't See My Mirrors, I Can't See You

Say this life rides on the back of a piebald mare.

Not mythic, not descended from Stonewall Jackson's mount.
Nobody's archetype.

Of course, there are props:
a little white dog with winged paws,
the plastic hibiscus.

In the background
a thematic hunger
no takeout can touch.

Time.
Time.
Feast and famine.

Say this ride is a mare.
You barely know
a hands-width
of her back.

We all say that this means that the world

A translation performance of Велимир Хлебников (Velimir Klebnikov)

This translation experiment regarding Velimir Klebnikov's poem "Out of the Bag" took place between April 21 and May 16, 2011, with the help of around 50 people in Berlin, as I walked around asking: *do you speak Russian?* And, *what does this mean?*

1) Out of a bag: To Klebnikov, start at Pasternak. I've got my Russian in the East Berlin restaurant. I need to know what this means. This means Out of a bag. This is all this means. *There is nothing else this could mean*. He offers no story. No stop-gapping. No emotional pause. No red-rover. No come on over. No question why. In striking confidence he tells me right away what this means without batting an, matter of, as if having saved these words from a fire, from forever, or longer, like every day, like every day of every year since his first color changing words. He has been waiting for nothing else his entire life but someone to ask what this means and today is the big what this means day. His friends agree. There is nothing else this could mean. It can only mean (1) Out of a bag. (2) Out of the bag. (3) From a bag where you keep your things. (4) From the purse you carry around. (5) From out of a sack. This is all this means. This is all this can mean and nothing else. There is no time for talk of containers and content, or interior deniers, or designers, or wheels and handles and straps, the possibilities of portability, the convenience of a table when needing to set things down. Now that I know what this means, I do not know what this means.

Out of a bag

2a) I am asked to trade my girl: What does this mean? A long streak of no's: *No, no, nein, no, nein, no, no, nee,* the eight people at the table say, one after the other like a stadium wave. *No. No one here speaks Russian,* the old Russian-looking man who is not Russian says, *but trade me your girl and I find you a Russian who can tell you what this means.* Should I take the question seriously? Can I trade my girl? For how long? What is fair trade? Will she be open-minded or thoughtless? Is this a no-brainer? I used to trade baseball cards and raw stones as old at the earth with fossils of first life. And I need that line. A girl for a line. My girl. I need to know what this means. She would trade me for a ripe squash, that's for sure. A stick of sage. A shoot of mint. A sprig of something for sprigging. A shoal of shallow water for lapping, or a shawl. Maybe they want a girl friend just as a friend? Maybe they were all traded for wild boars? Maybe they will trade my girl for a goat or a guy with a goatee or one of the Pleiades? Would I be trading up? Am I a trading-upper? I've never thought of myself as such. Could I keep the Russian line forever? Would it grow into a sunset or double rainbow? Would there be strict selection criteria in place by which I would know there is the possibility of improbable and radiantly enlivened things?

2b) I leave with All: A thick lognecked man planted outside, or perched, looking Russian, says, *without a doubt, I speak Russian and this is not Russian. Only the word* all *is Russian. The rest of this Russian is not Russian! Only the word* all *is Russian.* But it's from a Russian poet, I say. *This is not Russian! Do you speak Russian? I speak Russian! I can tell you, your Russian means nothing in Russian! This Russian means nothing in Russian! Only the word* all *is Russian. Only the word* all *is Russian.*

> Out of a bag
> all

2c) They say I no: A family of eight, of all ages, all eating, all laughing, all say: *no, I no, I no, I no, no, no, I no, I also no* Russian. One of the eight says, *I know Russia is only about 2000 kms that way. In Russia you'll find lots of Russians. There are lots of Russians in Russia who can help you with Russian.*

> Out of a bag
> all. I no

2d) Tactics I: (The toilet in the back): I ask in German for Russian. In English for Russian. In English to a Spaniard for Russian. In French for Russian. In English to a Turk for Russian in English. *Can you tell me what this means?*

In the evenings after work, while walking the dog, while shopping for eggs, while salivating for sun, while growing my invisible shield, while flying backwards forward, while knowing solve comes from *solvere* which means *to loosen* in Latin, while avoiding being fathomed, by the slowpokes and nay-sayers, by the sight seers, in the terraces of looks and tinsel, while meeting up for eating, and after the slaked drinking, the straw that reaches into your heart, and before home's weather, not having traded my girl, not thinking of forever, not using a pedocomparator, and before reading intimacy, and before the dreams obscured by sleep, I weave my way through the day's cafés and bars asking if anyone speaks Russian. I stew tactical turmoil. Lurk and listen. Nestle landfills. Squeeze scant strategies from surface distractions. Sing dimensions. Dear sir, *Is the toilet in the back? I lost my dog. I fell in love. I won the plums. I try a Russian translation! I call this world startling. I'll take the full boot too. By the way, have you heard anyone here speaking Russian today?* I have a secret message from, a missive to, a lost fragment that, a memory that needs, and. I get sharp at spotting sounds. At fabricating the instantaneous corridor. At the precise ecology of the temporary opening in the crowd. At the slip through spaces, at the Japanese *Ma*, at the instinct intertwined with intuition, and the precise interruptions. At the quick casual, *excuse me, I'm not from here. It's that way, yes. It's this way, thanks. It's back there, over here, around the last singing table, but please, do you know Russian? Do you read Russian? I need to know what this means. Can you help me find out what this means?*

2e) Tactics II: I rush in: I rush in to ask would be's be be's what this would mean in Russian. I listen everywhere. In the street I am listening. In the street I am listening. In the video store I am listening. I browse the Russian videos closely to find what is out. What is out? Is out in. I hide US films behind Russian films in the Russian film section, as I listen for Russian. I hang out in the bookstores. I check up on Chekov. I rack in the blouse stores, balance in the high-heel stores, suck in the tight pants stores (I don't mind the tight pants stores), trying to size up anyone speaking Russian. I slip into a hostel breakfast for youth. Clink on a water glass. Ask: does anyone here speak Russian? In the 5-star lobby, wearing a suit, before the manager spots my camouflage briefcase, with a manila folder under my arm, a heavy pen, an air of urgency, a confidence in vulnerability, wearing the look of someone invited, I announce my question, but no one knows what this means. Without having to take trains I stand by the trains waiting to hear Russians arriving and departing. Here I am, in a rush going nowhere. And then suddenly there are two. Out of the blue. And I rush into the train car, as if suddenly rushing will stop them from forgetting Russian. This means, something is spread around on the floor. The things fell down on the floor, and spread. And I am at peace for the time being.

> Out of a bag
> all. I no
> the things fell down on the floor, spread

3) I think 16 Turkish people come next: Six Turkish people in a park lunching on a blanket ask: *Why Russian? Why Russian? No, why? No why? Oh no. No. Ha ha ha, no.* The next eight Turkish people on the next blanket ask: *why?* Two Turkish people next to the two other blankets of Turkish people say, I think this means what comes next. I think this is what comes next. Yes. *Yes!* I say. *This must mean this. But why do you do this, they ask? You should do a Turkish poem, then we can all help tell you what things mean.* Next I will do a Turkish poem.

> Out of a bag
> all. I no
> the things fell down on the floor, spread
> what comes next

4) The People's Park: The next weekend in the Volks park no one speaks Russian. Outside the Volks theater, no one speaks Russian. In the lobby of the Volks theater, no one has heard anyone speaking Russian today. Back in the park he says, *no, I speak Italian*. She says, *No, English only*. In the café on the edge of the park they say, in order, from left to right, around in a circle —: *No, no, nee, nee, no, nee, nein. That felt very Russian*, the one says at the end. Two say twice each, *Why Russian? Why Russian? Why Russian? Why Russian?* Lots of people say, why Russian. *No, why, no, oh no, no why no, ha ha, no, of course not*, nodding her head no.

> *No, a little Polish.*
>
> *No, a little Greek.*
>
> *No, a little Spanish. So if you know you want to know what something means in what I speak I can tell you.*
>
> *No, just English.*
>
> *No, but many years ago*, six agree, *we knew Russian.*

Many now seem to say *many years ago*.
Finally six say this means: That the world. That the world. That
the world. That the world. That the world. That the world. If you
ask all of us, we will all say this means, that the world. But it's six
who all speak Russian! And I am so happy, me and my ecstatic
innards and this breeched infinitesimal yes want to hug them for
now speaking Russian in former East Berlin! *Thank you so much for
understanding what this means!*

> Out of a bag
> all. I no
> the things fell down on the floor, spread
> what comes next
> and the world

5a) Reading without understanding what you're reading: We all
speak *Finnish, and English, and German, and German, and German, and
German, and Danish, and Finnish, and English, and Sami. Some Ume
Saami, some Pite Sámi, some Lule Saame, and some Southern Samic, some
Inari Saamic, or Lappish and Lappic. But we all speak English now*, the
Finnish group says when they're finished. *But we can all read Rus-
sian, we just don't know what this means. Sorry, we just don't know what
this means.*

I ask a friend named Felix when the Finnish are finished.
Felix grew up in East Berlin. First Felix had to learn German, then
studied Russian, then added French, then added English, then
added Latin (Latin may have come before English), and is now
speaking English to me. We English the scary scene from *Middle-
march*. One morning, early in the time of courtship… "could I not
learn to read Latin and Greek aloud to you, as Milton's daughters
did to their father, without understanding what they read?" *Felix,
can you tell me what this means?* Felix says, *I can read Russian too, had
to as a kid, the Party things, but I just don't know what this means, same as
French, same as Latin. Well, when shit's written, shit does not smell*, Felix
says Barthes says Laporte says, say the translators.

5b) and 6) getting *warmer*: Two days later two people in a bread
line, first people of the day I ask, laugh and say, On the laughing.
Only something. The two people laugh and ask me why I ask them
if they speak Russian. They are not the first two people to laugh,

but they are the first people I've asked in three days who can read Russian and speak Russian and tell me in English or German what this means. So I laugh. And they laugh. And the three of us are laughing laughers laughing laughingly about this. So I ask the next line too, something I would not normally do, because it cuts down on the *differences which make a difference* factor. But I'm desperate because this is getting warmer. What getting warmer. Something in this direction, they say.

> Out of a bag
> all. I no
> the things fell down on the floor, spread
> what comes next
> and the world
> on the laughing, only something
> getting warmer

7) Near a grocery cart garden: I have one phrase left to reRussian. Alas, a dry spell. Alas, the word alas. At last at least twelve groups of people for two days say *no, no, no, no, no, no, no, no, no, no, no, no, no, no, no, no, no, no, no, no, no Russian.* Then I see Anastasia.

Anastasia's hanging out in FIT, *Freie internationale Tankstelle*, a gas station transformed into an open-air art project. She's making an empty grocery cart into a garden. Around 30 people are making empty grocery carts into gardens. I am told the grocery carts have been collected from all around Berlin. Turns out a type called a food artist, an urban systems planner, is holding workshops where everyone can learn how to make a mobile garden in anything that rolls. Eggs roll. Egg rolls. Language rolls. We roll. We can Wealcan—Old English *wealcan* "to toss, roll, to roll up, curl, to muffle up," from Proto-welk- Old Norse *valka* "to drag about," Danish *valke* "to full," Middle Dutch *walken* "to knead, press, full," Old High German meaning "to knead, to full"), perhaps ultimately from PIE root wel- (3) "to turn, roll" . . . So the pie rolls too. Anything goes. What kind of porous lining to use. How much and deep the mulch. Some signage for the seeds so people see there's something there growing. Roll the garden to a bleak and meager and desolate treeless plaza or street or parking lot. Bike-lock the garden to a lightpole or something. I know Anastasia will know what this means, Anastasia will know what this means. This means words from the mouth of a hanging person. The mute lip area. The living words that hang on a corpse. These mute words say a lot. But what odd words to use here. No one really uses the old words anymore.

The second original has begun. It has been three weeks. Three weeks for seven short lines. I want more. More laughter more trades more touching the world. I am not done Klebnikoving. I ask Anastasia, *where is the best place to go in Berlin where everyone still speaks Russian?* as I push a line of string-climbing bean seeds into the grocery cart mulch.

> Out of a bag
> all. I no
> the things fell down on the floor, spread
> what comes next:
> The world
> The laughing
> The getting warmer
> living words from the mouth of the dead man say a lot.

Kathryn Dunlevie, "Welcome to Planet Desire,"
mixed media on panel

The Worrier

hummingbird feeder

What comes near your door tonight?

A sound like feet balancing on stones.

A sound like something big
brushing through ferns.

Something is here to eat.

Does it come near your window?

It's the same bear.

Why do you think she has come?

She smells the popcorn.

What damage could she do?

She could lift the feeder
from its hook and drink.

Are you watching her?

Yes.

Where is she now?

She's below my kitchen window.

She's walking into my garden.

She's standing in the foxgloves.

Where is she now?

Rising to the jewel.

The Worrier
body

What is inside the sky?

The lavender of afterlife,
colander of rigatoni,
some butter of orange and mint.

What is inside the moon?

Two celadon plates,
old hemlock,
ice.

What is inside the stars?

A blender and a fire extinguisher.

A way of entering cutting board.
Two limes on the herringbone.

What is inside Venus?

A hatred of enamel.
The touch of minnows
at my ankles.

What is inside your silence?

An alcove of jackrabbits.
A Jeep door slamming.
The flat landscape of a lip.

What else does silence hold?

Billowing words,
blueberry sheets,
the failsafe,

the bitter scent of marigolds,
what I never said to my parents,
the flourishing, the flourishing,
the deadweight.

What is still pure?

Purity always waits
for a crime.

Purity scams.

The coverlet of waves.

And what is the purpose of waves?

They believe in the center.
They want to move.

What are the crimes of the lake?

Silence.
Not giving up the dead.
Grief.

And what does the lake heal?

Elbows of crawdads,
splintered oak,
edges of washed glass,
the plan of silver.

What does the silver do?

It allows the body
to surface.

The Worrier
photographers

Who is there?

The young neighbors with Emily the dachshund.
I share the garden with them, and the plum tree.

What do they shoot?

People in hazmat suits;
someone carrying an iPad
sweeping an old porch.

They take their photos on tintypes — collodions.

Why do they come to see you?

I keep treats for Emily.
I let them look through all my costumes.

No one else asks to see
what they see.

What do they tell you?

It took them seven hours to get it right —

the shadows kept changing, then it was a rush
to the dark-tent to wash the image in silver,

and the model then had to go
to her belly-dancing class.

What do they show you?

The collodion of that young woman
under the plum, in a huge wicker chair,

staring at a manikin on the ground, its plastic hand
in her lap, holding two broken cell phones,
telephone wires around her in a shawl.

What do they ask you for?

They ask me again to smell the lavender oil
that sets darkness on metal.

From the collection of the Senior Advisory Editor, photograph

Echo and the Domestic

Give me the double chocolate cake,
its layers with a few burnt pecans,
their conversation about lures
and whether they'll ever go
camping, about cutting that oak
to build a table. Give me
a cigar from Costa Rica,
an old pink robe I can slip into,
give me the ruby ring on granite,
the tray of matched earrings,
the moldy bit of Swiss in the cheese drawer,
give me the musk of a bedroom,
the sadness of perky breasts,
the promise of prescriptions,
give me the girl texting in gym class,
the cocky high school photo of the boy
with an overdose of facial jewelry.

Give me a shadow I can recognize,
which doesn't knock me back into the lake.

Give me the crow
to know what I feel and say it.

Give me any room, lavender with defiance.

Crow Evening

Crow watches blue-colored ice,

watches the eyelids of clouds blinking
open then closed.

And if a hole opens in the shallows
of a distant pond, swallowing a young boy,

Crow has no opinion beyond the wind,
beyond breath that lifts

a chest then knocks it down.
And everywhere are the sounds of native

tongues, the mother calling
from the back porch, the emptiness

of syllables in air. Crow doesn't
imagine that it matters. Crow has the memory

of the boy sinking out of sight, the pond
with its open black wound.

Crow has the gray sun behind the clouds,
the snow beginning to form and fall.

Crow dreams of the red sun of summer,
the rising moon with its blood-wet eye.

Lost: A Sister's Tale

Adapted from the Grimms' tale, "The Seven Ravens"

Four black hawks circle the freeway at twilight
like the four lost brothers of a girl
walking across the fields

carrying her mother's ring tied to a handkerchief
a wooden stool, a loaf of bread
a pitcher of water to ease thirst.

So hard to keep an eye on her stumbling
through fallow fields, overgrown forests
even her brothers lose sight of her.

They beat their wings
cry their hoarse signal *kri-i, kri-i*

sister, sister in dark syllables
during their hunting hour

when rabbits and voles browse
the rustling grass and bits of violet cloud
break off to drift over eastern mountains.

They hover above and you
crane your neck as the sky
sucks you into blue

so high you forget where that girl was born,
in what century, country, village,
what your name was

the taste of your mother's bread, and this
longing that swallows all others.

The oldest brother breaks the circle
heading east and pulls the others, weaving
black and gold behind them.

Do they spot you, or some
crooked branch, twitching shadow?

Stygian wings streak the vineyard kingdom
of crows into blue hills and you wonder
if you'll reach the edge of the world

and enter the cavern
where hawk brothers sleep,

if you'll have time for a sip of wine
from each of four beakers, time to slip
your mother's ring into the last of them.

In which country has she left
her cumbersome stool, where is your cup?

When four hawks cleave the evening sky
and disappear, the air vibrates leave-taking.

Eleanor Leonne Bennett, photograph

Burnt Dress

Even in old age I need you—
your voice, a ripple of waves
across a bare field tracked
by the capricious ash-gray hare.

Forgive me if I chant your name
to drive my fears into daylight.
I am an angel in a burnt dress.

Beauty walks this world aging everything—
each colonnade, leaf, sparrow,
lintel, scarf, water bird.

I call you now from the square,
stalls hung with yellow roses and handbags.
So much stone here,
a starfall of stained glass.

Your words sprout
from my heart like mallow.
You tell me to claim
the wildness I once wanted.

Pared to the least
of morning's blossom, bird,
my breath
spread so thin that nothing's
left but bone
white emptiness,
whisper of ruins.

Or one egret in a field.
The loneliness
of angels without
even the body of a shadow.

Passing, forever passing
into and out of this world.

Closing In

for Jeremy

The dog barks at the wind's dark.
My heart breaks in half
the fall you leave home.

How does any mother
bear this?
When I was young,

my teacher scolded:
Just describe the cup.
Don't describe your feelings

about the cup.
Thirty years later

I still can't contain
myself. I am
the cup,

the cup that kept you.
Your dog's no dummy.
The dark is deep.

Dutch Translation

A painting is nothing but daubs on canvas.
A photo—only a puppet theater
play of light and shadow.
A poem—black scratches on paper
like rows of stitches on a quilt of snow.

But the ladies in the National Gallery
crowd closer, as though Vermeer's
domestic interior were a showhouse
To Let in a Dublin suburb, a place
they might imagine as their own.

Coffee in the morning with *The Irish Times*,
the sheen of rain on a slate roof.
Light entering through net curtains,
obsidian glimmer of a leather sofa.
Persian rug, pearl earring.

Kim Bultman, "Coffee for Two," photograph

Accompanying Anne Carson in "The Fall of Rome"

"Almost *decaf* in the glare of the white sand ahead,"
I read. But she has written "almost *deaf*" —
can't you hear it? how a c enters to swallow
the fear? She's writing about death,
the stranger we concoct against
while drinking Nescafé. It's the end of her
32-page poem, 5 lines to go, and she is
leaving with so much energy and wit, she has
put a c in my eyes as if never to go
blind. Or deaf for that matter.
It feels good to be part of someone substantial,
to take the unknown by the handle
of its cup and pour warmth (albeit specious)
into the void which comes after dessert.

Pit Bulls

It's like she smells real dark somehow. Kind of musty and sweet and almost bad. But good. Real good. I never knew that smell could matter. It's faces and bodies that me and my friends are always looking at and talking about. Not smell.

But so sweet, so dark.

"Right there," she's saying and I've got my mouth on her ear. I never knew that either, that you could bite an ear. Kiss her, get her into bed. That's what we'd always said.

"When do your parents get home?" she's asking.

I look at the clock on the nightstand and tell her pretty soon.

"I have to go then," she says.

I'm on top of her on my small bed and don't move because I know there's lots of time and it just feels real good to be with her. She's smiling and maybe trying to move away but mostly just smiling.

"I have to go, Jimmy," she says in a few minutes and this time I move.

She stands and buttons her shirt and puts on her jacket.

"I'll see you tomorrow in class," she says when we're downstairs and she's opened the front door.

The sun's shining on the concrete porch and I'm standing near the door, slowly scraping at the paint that's flaking off. She walks out and I grab her hand and pull her back inside, into the shade of the entryway, and I'm kissing her.

And she's against me and I can see the neighbor's house across the street and their pit bull hanging in the front yard, its jaw locked onto an old tire that's hanging from a tree. It's hanging there like it was when I let Lara in, hanging there like it always does.

Lara's skin, in the light, it turns brown, like her eyes, a black girl. How is it that I'm here with this black girl?

And I see that pit bull and for a second I think there's someone there, on the porch behind the pit bull, watching us, seeing us. But there isn't.

❖ ❖ ❖

In the morning I'm standing on the porch waiting for my ride to school. There's dew on the table and chairs that my dad and brother made when I was a kid and I can see my breath. But the sky's real blue and you can feel how it's not cold like winter anymore, how it'll be warm by afternoon. There are old newspapers stacked on the porch and I take one and lay it on the painted concrete steps to sit on.

Across the street I see that pit bull walking around its yard and in its mouth is this cat. The dog is pure white but there's blood on its face and chest.

That dog's always getting out and killing cats and it's even killed a couple dogs down the street. Big dogs, like a German Shepherd and a Doberman.

I've played with that pit bull in its yard. The owner was there and I don't think I've ever met a nicer dog. All that pit bull wanted was to lick my face and lay on top of me. He wagged his tail like some dog in a cartoon and I petted him and let him lick my hands and face. He'd press against me and that white fur was so soft and underneath there was muscle that was as hard as wood and I looked around to see if the owner was still there.

I'm looking at the blood on its face as it rubs its rib cage hard against the chainlink fence.

I'm wondering whose cat got killed. Maybe someone's dog.

It's jumping for the tire and now I see it drops the pieces of the cat and I get a shiver and can see my breath again. I stand and walk toward the street, wondering if it comes quick, if there's a snap inside and those dogs kill. Biting without knowing, killing without realizing, knowing it only when there's blood and there's the taste and the smell.

Five feet in the air that dog jumps and it catches that tire with its mouth and it's shaking and swinging and hitting hard and loud against the fence. The blood's all down its neck and there's saliva spraying out from its mouth and I'm wondering if that pit bull ever feels regret.

I'm sure that pit bull will be dead soon. Tacoma's a place where people take their dogs seriously.

❊ ❊ ❊

English is my last class and it's in a room that's always too hot or too cold and it's taught by a teacher who likes to talk about his shoes and his dog.

This is why we met, I think. I don't know any other way we would have. We sit next to each other and I started looking at her. There was nothing else to do. Sometimes she'd be looking at me and after a while we started talking and after a while longer we started touching. Not clearly or openly. Just reaching for a pencil, borrowing a book. Touching a hand, touching a leg. Making sure no one saw.

Even now we don't see each other anywhere else at school. We have different friends, we do different things.

Today the room's so hot. I can hear the heater humming behind me and can see the sun outside and here's this teacher up front talking about his little dachshund.

I sit here and feel the heat from behind me and can see Lara without her shirt on and can feel her skin against my hand. And I can smell her, even there, in class, when no one else could ever smell it.

❖ ❖ ❖

I get home from school and sit down on the porch and I'm looking over at the O'Connells' house next door. I can see the older neighbor girl doing something on the porch.

"You're just watching that white girl like she can't even see you, aren't you?" says Lara, surprising me, and I turn and she's my girlfriend. I'd never thought of that before.

"All you boys are the same," she says. And she's smiling and I'm scared in a way and she's my girlfriend.

I look across the street and see that pit bull standing at the fence, looking over at us.

"It's not like you touched her," Lara says and sits next to me.

"I used to look up at her window," I say. I'm talking slowly but I feel myself smiling a little. The pit bull turns away from the fence. "When I was a kid," I say. "I'd hope she was there and maybe I'd see something."

Lara looks over at the neighbor girl. "She ain't got nothing," she says. I'm thinking she'd sit that way, smiling like that, all day and be happy. And if she did sit there all day, it'd make me happy too.

"Wanna go to the store?" she says. She's staring at me and smiling and it's almost like she's studying something. "I got my dad's truck and I thought I'd go to the store." She waits a moment. "I parked it around the corner."

"Yeah," I say and I touch her hand.

"It's about time you touched me," she says.

Her dad's truck is nice. It's red and clean and new.

"We're going to Megafoods," she says when we're inside the truck. "I like Megafoods," she says. "And it's way out in the suburbs."

She turns the key and there's music on the radio that I've never heard. I reach to change the station but stop.

"No rock and roll," she says and for a second it's like I've been caught at something. But she's smiling. "My daddy's truck doesn't get rock and roll."

❊   ❊   ❊

Megafoods is as big as a warehouse and has food stacked almost to the ceiling in big cardboard shipping boxes. There are forklifts to reach up high and music's playing. The lights are bright and they reflect off the floor and the colored packages on the lower shelves.

We're in the frozen food section and Lara's holding a can of Coke in her hand. I'm eating a plum.

"I like this place," Lara is saying.

She drinks from the can.

"Does your mom shop here?" she asks me.

I shake my head.

"No, neither does mine. I tell her I'd go shopping with her if she did. Maybe that's why she doesn't." Lara's laughing at that and I'm not sure why. "Look at that bag of dog food," she says. "That bag's as big as me. Who needs that much dog food?"

"My neighbor," I say.

"That dog's evil. You can see it."

"I played with it once," I say. "It was so nice."

She drinks, her mouth damp, then says, "It's still evil."

We stop at the end of the aisle and Lara's looking up and trying to read the signs at the ends of the other aisles. She steps away from me and I'm watching her and thinking that it's like she fills up so much space, like this place or any place was waiting for her.

"What are we looking for here, anyway?" I ask her.

"I don't know," she says and reaches for my hand. "Maybe some donuts," she says and she's smiling and leading me down another aisle.

❈ ❈ ❈

In the kitchen I'm helping my mother with the dishes. I have a beer behind the toaster that I drink from when she's not looking. Not that she doesn't know it's there. She just doesn't want me to show that it's there.

My brother comes into the kitchen and I take a drink from my beer. Mark is nineteen and has his own apartment now, after he got a good job at a lumber yard out in the suburbs. He's just here for dinner. He's about a foot taller than my mother and he's just standing next to her looking down as she wraps food in foil.

"Let me help you there, Mom," he says, joking, and he's sort of holding her arms as she tries to cover up some potatoes. "You got to wrap it real tight," he's saying as he leans against her. "No, no, yeah," he's saying and she's smiling and trying to ignore him.

"Just leave me alone, Mark," she's saying and trying to pull away from his hands, but she's still smiling.

"I'm just helping, Mom," he says and I lean against the counter and take a drink from my beer. They'll do this for a while, Mark smiling and getting in her way and my mother not even looking up at him, trying to ignore it.

"You're very cute," my mother says quietly and Mark's reaching over her shoulders and holding a salad bowl in front of her.

"No, really, yeah," he's saying. "Like that, yeah, no, okay Mom, here we go, just trying to help."

I'm smiling because they always do this. I do it too sometimes. But only when Mark's here. It's Mark's thing.

After a few minutes she gets the bowl into the refrigerator and Mark is leaning against the counter, smiling like he's proud of himself.

"You know Jimmy's dating a nigger," Mark says.

I'm staring at him and he's looking at my mother. She's holding a plate and looking back at him.

"Don't say nigger," she says.

"Well, he is," Mark says and he's still smiling. "It's not a big deal. I thought about doing it too but never did."

I open the refrigerator and take out a beer and see her watching me.

"Don't say nigger," she says, still looking at me.

"Okay. Black girl. He's dating a negro," he says. "I wish I would have. Really. I do."

I take a drink and watch my mother and don't look at him.

"Don't tell your father," she says looking at him. "Don't say black girl, don't say negro, don't say nigger."

"It's not like he loves her. It's not like it's a serious thing he's got with her."

I take a drink and now she's watching me.

＊　＊　＊

Lara's here, in my room.

It's after school and she came over. She's nervous, I'm thinking. She's thinking about something else.

"Why do I like you?" she says. Her voice isn't nervous.

"I don't know," I say. I'm leaning against my window sill. I haven't touched her. I didn't know she was coming.

She steps closer and is kissing me and there's that smell. So sweet. So nice. I'm touching her, I have my hand in her shirt. I don't like it there, I'm thinking. Don't have your hand there.

I hear something banging outside and she opens up my shirt and I've got her shirt open and her bra open and there's something still banging outside. I can hear it. And it's so warm against her and it's so soft and there's that smell and I think I can feel it banging, I think I can feel it hitting me.

And I'm saying things to myself that I don't want to be saying.

She has my hand and she presses it against her jeans. "No," she's saying and her voice is nervous. "Keep it there," she is saying. I'd put my hand there and didn't know it and she wants it there.

And the button's open and the zipper's down and it's the pit bull outside. It's the pit bull hanging from the tire and swinging against the fence.

And now it's so warm.

She has me on the bed and I'm pulling off her jeans. I hear her breathing and then she stops and things are so tight and smooth and I hear her voice and see her there. So brown. Beautiful.

It's all very beautiful.

And I feel the bedspread. I'm done. It's not so warm. My back even feels kind of cold. Her skin is damp. My face is in her neck. Part of me feels bad. Like I didn't do it right.

After a minute I raise my head and she's staring at me. I hear the pit bull hitting the fence outside.

I kiss her. I close my eyes.

Black girl, negro, nigger.

We get dressed and she's saying something. "Coming home soon," I'm saying. I feel bad. I want her to leave. I want to do it over. I want to forget how I did it.

"I'll see you in English," she's saying and the front door's open and I see the pit bull drop from the tire and run to the fence to watch me.

I close my eyes.

Black girl, negro, nigger.

*   *   *

It starts to rain. It's gray this morning and cold. I walk down the steps to let the rain fall on my hair and face.

I'm tired. I don't want to go to school today.

The pit bull walks around the corner of our house. I think to run and don't. But I look and it's got blood down its back leg and it's limping bad, walking slow and kind of sideways.

It looks up at me and its jaw is turned down and bleeding and I look away. It's whining quietly and choking a little and pushing its side against my leg. I reach down and pet it and wipe rain from my face with my other hand. Petting its neck and back and I don't mind the blood so long as I don't see that mouth or jaw. The dog's breathing and it sits down and it's still crying quietly.

I slide my hand along its wet fur. I can see its leg and the hole from the bullet.

My brother is picking me up this morning. He'll come and we'll get the gun from our dad's room.

I'm thinking about how I slept badly.

The dog turns its head and pushes its mouth against my arm like it's trying to lick me. I pull away slowly and can see the blood on my jacket and the dog follows my arm with its mouth. And I just let it have the arm, let it try to lick it.

But then I watch for a few minutes and see the dog's mouth and that pit bull's not trying to lick me. It's crying and its jaw won't move but it's trying to bite me.

Lara walks up. "I've got my dad's truck again," she says, then sees the dog and all the blood and she's staring down at that dog.

I think she'll scream a little or jump away, but she just stares down at that dog.

"Dog got shot," she says.

I nod.

"Does your daddy have a gun?" she asks.

It's a moment before I nod. The dog is still pressed against me and I try to push it away. The dog growls at me and Lara slides between me and the dog, the dog now pushing at her.

I go inside and get the .38 from my dad's cabinet. When I get back outside, Lara's sitting, the dog leaning forward on her, blood all over her arms and lap. She's staring into its face.

"Bad dog," she's saying quietly. "You're a bad, bad dog."

The gun is not that heavy, but it's cold in the air outside.

Lara stands up and moves away. The dog tries to follow her but she points at it, hand up, staring into its eyes. She says, "Stay."

I shoot it in the head.

It takes a few minutes for the two of us to drag the body over to the neighbor's house. We press it up against the fence.

We're both covered in blood.

"I was going to give you a ride," she says. "But now I need to go back home."

I nod.

She's staring at me.

"Now is when you touch me," she says.

I nod.

"On the hand," she says. "Or lean out to kiss me."

I touch her hand.

"This is when you tell me you'll go get changed and come with me," she says. "Come with me to my house."

I nod. I'm still holding her hand.

"Before we go to school," she says, staring at me, smiling slightly. "Right?"

"Yes," I say. "Right," I say.

"You're coming with me," she says, but it's a question also.

"Yes," I say, and I'm close to her now. "Yes."

Christopher Woods, "The Dreaming House," photograph

Affirmation

It's not that the bullet doesn't love what it strikes —
that briefest penetration that changes
the make-up of flesh forever.
Are we not all married to what completes us?

After spiraling half a lifetime through the vacuum
of cool metal chambers
awaiting that promised purpose,
imagine being pushed by fire
out into being —
how would you not rejoice?
How would you not find everything affirmed,
that yes you exist alongside the sun,
yes your life bears consequence
and bleeds into tomorrow —

to be just one
of the tangled knots in humanity,
devoted to that misunderstood
sacrificial path.

Allow

Do not give me paraphrase.
Do not settle and sift,
leave me without recourse,
my brick tears stacking a wall.

Allow chinks where light
might ooze in. Allow syllables
to muster and cling, find
sense and delicious nonsense, both.

Do not feign or tell me tales
so tall they tickle the clouds.
Do not pretend there is love in the room.
The spin has sucked out all the air.

Let time be threaded with more
than lies, perhaps a measure of music,
or seeds for columbine and rue.
Allow me scissors for the fossil moon.
Allow me vestiges and folly.

Argiope, Goddess of Small Repute

If I were a goddess of even small repute,
I would take my cues from Argiope,
spider of garden and fencerow.
I would not scuttle away
like some brown recluse
from the lover who spurned me. I'd
paint my face silver! wear robes of ebony
and gold, throw the drapes open wide, slay
snapping turtles for soup —

                       And if I got rousted
by things unseen or seen, you would not
catch me admitting doubt.

                    Still, of extravagant
quiet, of old dramas writ small, Argiope
makes room on the flesh of her back
for yellow sun and black earth to settle
their differences. Between yarrow and golden rod,
she paces off coordinates on x and y, in her spiral
writes a gospel of rivet and weld.
When the vowels of summer plainsong
lean into her web — *Dominus Exsultemus,*
In Paradisum angeli — they bow
but do not break it. Her eight legs comb
the space between tones, they groom
the counsel that keeps her. And when
some errant grasshopper thrills her web with banjo twang,
she restores all stillness with a bite.
       She of extravagant reach
       is no less chaste than a circle in a square —

                          If
I were a goddess of even small repute
I'd do well to take cues from Argiope:
       Travel light, mind where I step,
       make a new web tomorrow
       from the web I eat today. And before
       I forgive me my trespasses,
       measure twice.

Vámonos de nuevo

Tierra húmeda y negra de las barrancas
y raíces, al lado mismo del agua.
—Saltos sobre las piedras
y remolinos
hay hojas de navegantes
y brillo, y frío—.

Una piedra lustrosa, negra y lisa
un reflejo de troncos, de pastos altos
de ramas finas
y una voz rumorosa de vientos en hojas
diciendo algo confuso, sobre nuestras cabezas.

Flores muy chicas
con pétalos que arrojan un rojo vivo
y casi alumbran

Alas de insectos
de un celeste que casi no es color, transparente
tiemblan, se agitan.

Y aquel rumor de monte, de vida múltiple
latiendo en cada hueco, en cada grieta,
aquel ruido de viento, de agua
de pájaros alzando el vuelo
con un golpe de ala y grito áspero.

Let's Go Again

Damp black earth of the riverbanks
and roots, by the same side of the river.
—Jumping over the stones
and eddies
there are leaves sailing,
and brightness, and cold—.

A lustrous stone, black and smooth
a reflection of the tree trunks, tall grass
thin branches
and a rumor of wind in the leaves
saying something confusing, over our heads.

Tiny flowers
with petals a vivid red
that almost catch fire.

Wings of insects
a sky blue that is almost not a color, transparent,
tremble, flutter.

And that murmur of a hill, of many lives
beating in each hollow, in each crevice
in each rush of wind, of water,
of birds taking flight
with a beating of wings and a harsh cry.

Translated from the Spanish by Jesse Lee Kercheval

Foldings

Packing for his return to England, Grandfather showed me how to roll socks into little fists, tuck them into shoes, fold shirts into rectangles tidy as sealed envelopes. I was three. His suitcase a marvel of geometric shapes, not a sliver of wasted space. Key twisted in the suitcase lock.

I'm folding sheets now, smoothing squares into smaller squares so they'll nestle at right angles on the linen closet shelf. I was six when Granny showed me how to iron without an iron, "finger pressing," she called it. How to smooth the wrinkled, still-damp fabric of a skirt or blouse with the flat of your hands.

In my twenties when Mom called, took a half-hour to tell me what she'd hidden so far down in a drawer it had taken decades to find. She said she'd finally remembered: nighttimes, in the big bed, her little-girl self folded between them, her daddy played with her, taught her to play with him, her mummy right there.

How you can fold yourself in on yourself. The toes of the socks curl innermost, the tops wrapping around them. How you can take your own layers and tuck them into creases.

Grandfather's origami — on his second visit, he showed us how to fold a piece of plain white paper into tiny triangles, and then — voilà! — open a flower, a bird.

After Mom's phone call I lay down on my own bed. Over and over I said to myself, "Mom's going to be all right, now Mom's going to be okay."

Forty years later, last summer in Paris, at the Centre Pompidou — the paintings of Simon Hantaï, wide white walls with his room-sized unfoldings. He'd crushed the canvases, folded the cloth so he couldn't see the whole surface while he brushed the paint. Pliage. Said he didn't want to know where the edge was, where the canvas stopped.

A different kind of folding. And unfolding. The way you shake a clean sheet 'til it sails over the bed, billows. The way a white-winged dove folds her wings close to her rounded middle, then opens them out, lifts off. Unfoldings, the way a flock of swallows makes pinpricks in the sky, openings. Rents in a reddening evening.

Glenn Herbert Davis, photograph

Rapunzel, Unshorn

For seven years hope was the song
I longed to hear: shears humming,
the purr of ribbons and bows as each braid let loose
its seamless ladder. After smuggling me in,
the crone learned to soon rid the room
of anything sharp — stones, nails,
the splintered grin from a ruined saucer —
leaving as solace a single window,
shatterproof and framed in ivory.
On those nights when her skirts hissed
like scissors up the stairs, my hair
became a bed we shared, her body tamped
to mine, haloing us both
in gold. I never called her mother,
not when I had my own to imagine,
the myth of her abiding far
from where the moon combed over
my prison of brick and stone.
In dreams, I gave her hands
that nested inside sleeves like little birds,
lips the crimson of pinched berries.
It was only her voice which soothed
the evening air — primrose brewed
with a brush of lavender along
the ear, not the reek of river sludge,
willow-thin and creased with silt,
a stench strong enough to stir
me from dream and back to the scalp
pressed cool against my neck,
pocked and unspoiled by curls.
This close, I recognized beneath
her apron the rough language of rope,
her talon's rigid grip. Desire
was a static in the heart already exposed,
but it was never her I feared, only
what I was always denied, my ever-after
a burden she preserved. An ornament

spangling at dawn the garden where she roamed
barefoot among rows and rows of rampion,
her mouth a soundless pucker as she knelt
to the earth, caressed each head
like a newborn—tender, budding,
their dreams still rooted in darkness.

From the collection of the Senior Advisory Editor, photograph

Alone at Night

All stillness suspect, the hallway
dim, an open casket, the kitchen
clutching its knives. I turn
on every single light & triple-check
the locked front door.

All those women pinned to the floor.

Roi J. Tamkin, photograph

Babysitting

In their bedroom, her dusty heels roost
in the closet, the lacy tongue of a garter belt
flashes its clasp from a half-shut drawer.
On bent hangers his undershirts wrinkle and stare,
and I suddenly remember why I'm here.

Shadows slide from the crib when I crack the door.
Love is as quiet as this, as blameless as a broken kite.
I'm careful not to wake the sleeping form.

Ovid in Exile

At first you kept a calendar, counted days.
But for months seagulls swabbed the same horizon,
and when winter came, the innkeeper, laughing,
peeled back your wineskin's leather to show you

the frozen shape: red and grooved as the shoulder
of a skinned deer. *I change into something poor and strange,*
you wrote. And your letters changed
from pleas to come home into long goodbyes,

as ships gathered like mourners in the harbor,
waves shoveling the deepening sky.

Sheila Cantrell, "Eastward Shell," graphite on paper

Ghazal

This is how you take your life.
Marry one, loving another.

Is this how we got smarter?
Eaten by one, eating another.

These are life's only chances.
God is one, dying another.

This life comes in two acts.
Sleeping one, waking another.

No man is an island entire: you
Are one, becoming another.

Shahid, is this your luck in life?
Living one, wasting another.

Waiting

It is a woman's start in life
to keep the world waiting,
to slow down the clocks
'til seconds move like hours,
'til each seed becomes a tree,
'til each drop goes out to sea,
'til each man, strong in his prime,
grows old through the quality
of waiting—eternally—for you.

Shoshana Kertesz, photograph

Scheherazade

They were raised
as if feral by nuns, fed at the back door. My mother chain-smoked
Lucky Strikes, ironed clothes in her robe, told me stories,
family yore, outlasted another night.

Penny,
she said, was the next-to-the-youngest, danced *adagio* in nightclub dives,
lived with a man who beat her, wanted to pimp her,
met a good man, wed him on her deathbed at thirty-four.

Rita
found religion, lived it, thrived, children twined around her
like clematis vines. She chose to ignore her church's insistence
on brimstone and blaming.

Gen,
an artist, jumped from a tenement fire—her child stopped breathing
in her arms. She coddled a bottle of gin all years after. Each
canvas throbbed, re-learning color.

Dot,
whip-tongued, funny, smart, married often, died rich,
but still gleaned from thrift-shop bins. She fought off whiskey,
loved her daughters with fierce pain.

When clouds
buckled, rained ice, my mother, the eldest, held them all,
rocked them, crooned tales, rhymes,
untangled their hair.

I dream them
on my porch, fat as neutered cats, content, sun
on their backs, out-staring time,
food on a flowered dish.

Reading A Child's Christmas in Wales

It is evening.
Three generations sit down in a living room
littered with the flotsam of Christmas day.
This year
there is a new baby
and a newly divorced neighbor,
her first Christmas alone.
I extract a half-eaten candy cane
wedged between two couch pillows
before I take my place next to the six-year-old.
Last year
she couldn't have navigated Hop On Pop.
Now she sails through the first page of the poem,
including the lines:
*"I could never remember whether it snowed for six days and six nights when I was twelve
or whether it snowed for twelve days and twelve nights when I was six."*
She is as untroubled by the skimpy punctuation
and quirky syntax
as the next reader, her dentist grandfather, is troubled by it.
The Welshman's words are passed from hand to hand around the room,
now intoned with a thick south Boston accent,
now in a voice muddled by wine and riches,
and by minds just struggling to take hold
of the strange meanderings
of another man's mind.
I love this poem,
and it doesn't matter at all what happens
because it is true
the words need us,
need us to form them again in our clumsy mouths,
swaddling them with our thick tongues
bringing them forth,
words
that are but remnants of another man's memories
wondrously imagined.
Murmured together,
they become our own memories.

It doesn't matter
that the words dissolve
the instant they are spoken
like snowflakes falling on the Welsh sea.

The little dog-eared red book travels around the circle.
We read our treasured pages
as some of us have done
nearly every Christmas for forty years
in other rooms
now inhabited by strangers.
The last reader closes the book.
The room is silent for a few moments
except for the overtones
of other voices
sounding beyond our walls.
The neighbor wipes away a tear
and gets up to start on the dishes.
Someone pops a bottle,
the baby grows restless,
his mother
wraps him in a blanket
and walks him slowly around the room.

Eleanor Leonne Bennett, photograph

Stepbrother

Got a ride from a Hall of Fame sportswriter
west on New York Thruway blinking into sun
told me Casey had forgotten more baseball
than Ralph Houk ever knew, but the trouble was

he had forgotten it — I was traveling
by way of women and song to Ithaca
to show up for Cy's Cornell graduation
slept for 24 hours once I got there

Cy and I hiked near Mount Diablo the day
before his father, my stepfather, passed away
we toked on an outcrop, I wrote a poem

about stones and bones — Cy commented that his
poem would have been about the two of us —
brother unbrother, unforgotten, unknown.

Glenn Herbert Davis, photograph

Ancient Peoples

The gods roll the sun into the sky,
fill the rivers, dump in the fish,
inflate the clouds, hand-operate
the animals and finally settle
on who gets a bombshell
and who gets a breather

Down below, while the vendors
curse each other, newlyweds stroll
the fruit stalls and buy a pomegranate
hoping the wet seeds will ignite
a pregnancy

A man is cleaning clay
from his nails with a broken
reed and a woman is praying
to every known and unknown god
for the absolution of sins
she's not sure she committed

No one is thinking about
becoming an ancient people
or what big deals they'd be
for coming up with writing,
not to mention the 60-second
minute or the razor

No one is thinking about
their bowls and beads
or that receipt for three goats
showing up in a glass case
in 5,000 years

Or how someone from the future
will imagine that boy tossing
a melon down the steps,
the shadow of a fern
on mudbrick eclipsed
by the sudden swing
of his mother's hand.

Martin Luther, Plagued in His Retirement by Sickness, Appeals to His Wife

Wittenberg, Germany, 1536

I am confounded, Katie, that my heart,
aflutter like a candle flame, misbehaves
even here in our Eden of plenty, my cart
of beans, lettuces, and the cloven halves

of African watermelons our sons severed
in outright deviltry, too cumbrous for me
to push on this miry path. Am I embittered
by my ills? No, for the Lord God gave me

you. And you, my Lord Katie, shall salve
my heart tonight with your newest physic
of garlic, hawthorn, and onion. You saved
yourself years ago from your monastic

life by fleeing in a pickled herring barrel.
Do no less for me, love, in my peril.

Lord Katie, Three Days Before Christmas

Wittenberg, Germany, 1540

I have milked dear Biene and Liebling until
their udders are dry as Christmas stollen left
too long in the hearth oven, its raisin fill
akin to year-old rat dung . . . . Martin! Lift

the Yule tree onto the board so I may place
a linden crown and the last few Blaunderelly
apples on it . . . Paul, help your Papa pace
himself, or there will be no salted pork belly

bacon in the skillet for you! And pen the dog
and the cock in the yard—for Heaven's sake,
child, latch the door! I hear, son, in Prague
a boy's shoes are filled with twigs if he takes

Jesus' name in vain . . . . Your tongue, Martin,
is huge, and speckled red. Let *me* say matins . . .

The Presbyterian Minister, Donald Cargill, to His Dead Wife on the Eve of His Execution

Edinburgh, July 26th, 1681

Ah, sweet Margaret, how Sirius, our Dog Star,
visible, nay ghostly, through this leaded pane,
assuages my ache tonight. Think how far,
love, its light reigns. I shall not abstain

from speaking here of my death, or its ambit.
The King's Privy Council has found me guilty
of treason, and early on the morrow a gibbet,
arisen at the mercat cross, will claim me.

But first, to the throng, I shall repeat my plea
that no man has leave to dictate God's design.
Then, Margaret, at last my soul may flee
this earthly life, and will, like a lantern

at dusk, or Canis Major, now vaporous blue,
limn the light of heaven as I rejoin you.

Poem in Which I Nearly Fail to Be Mentioned [Week Twenty]

The state funeral drones on
with its cerebrum-cracking
fanfares, its martial precision,
vexillar semiotics clear as
pebbles at the bottom of a river,
smooth as ritual choreographed
to march its way, image by image,
shot by calculated shot into
the double-edged platitude
of our collective memory.

Little boy saluting his father's
casket. Dutiful wife laying
head upon the fine oak box
containing the bones she served,
one way or another, for most
of her life. To the dead we give
their just honors; like Tobit
we must pay respects to any
body we encounter, us or them,
known or not, good or bad.

But still, what of the statue
of Reason and Irreligion marched
up to the altar of Notre Dame,
the flag raised over a so-called
Christian nation, when the birds,
the birds, who's even asked what
their religious affiliation is?
And the possums? From their babies,
I'd say Catholic or Orthodox,
but from their faces a religion
opaque enough to frighten the bejezus,
their faces un-me enough to stir
something in me like a stone.

How can I sing of this place without turning
red, without turning around the verses,
giving you something I said I wouldn't?
Everything gets clothed in something else,
the incense burning not as offering, but
as perfume, the child screaming on the way
to the idol, child screaming, being born.

Eleanor Leonne Bennett, photograph

Crown to Rump *[Ultrasound]*

at this point
we are all
the same: mom
with jellied
belly; inside,
banded screen
gives glimpse
of novelty,
eyeful of new,
you monochrome,
you suspended,
you in your sac,
you asleep.

Velvet

In synagogue in the suburbs, we fill with song in book after book and the Tigris rises up and makes a blessing. We are in our seats, running our hands on the velvet beside us. Our mouths are moving. Our eyes are down.

There is one story and one story, and we repeat it each week. This story is true and foolish. Words huddle, back to front, with occasional laments and long echo. We are waiting to learn about today, tomorrow, why we must suffer. I am wearing a white dress, my father a tie.

Even at this moment, the river insists on flowing. I smell the perfume of the desert. Old men advance with their widening language, pushing carts, selling words without farewell, without salt, without the flesh of worry. Silver birds quiver in the sun.

Then, I'm not at the water. The sermon has ended. There are round tables of bread on old platters. My father laughs, his cheeks like globes. A day of rest. All day we are lucky.

Dinner Party

Sunset settles on the roof of the house
in the guise of a female cardinal. Dull gray

laundry in the dryer,
hardwood floor swept clean. I set

six glasses out,
lay forks with tarnished tines.

This morning I deprived the tulips
of water, to tinge their petals brown,

steeped the linens in assamese ceylon tea.
When getting the olives out,

I see my face in the stainless
door of the fridge

is not my face.
The weight of the bird makes my bones ache.

The remnant of last month's moon
is trapped like a rag in my claws.

My husband greets guests, fills glasses
with wine, while the sun nests

in the tinder-dry bark
of the eucalyptus trees.

In the Shadow of Masters

Cairo, 1981

Om Reda sauntered past jasmine shrubs and palm trees, enjoying the bustle of cars and rickshaws on Cupola Street. She turned at a corner, walked a short distance to creaking metal gates and stepped into an alley. Finally, she entered the turn-of-the-nineteenth-century apartment building where she worked as a maid.

She plodded on worn marble steps to the third floor, rubbing bruises at her elbows. She sighed, remembering the joy she felt when her son was born twenty years ago, before his temper tattooed her arms. Following his birth, people renamed her the mother of Reda; *Om Reda* was the sweetest sound.

A stray cat rushed by, her gray fur rubbing Om Reda's ankles. "Come back, you little *Meow*. I'll give you treats." She rang the doorbell and saw Fatima's gangly shadow through the frosted panels. Om Reda smiled at the woman who was docile as a child due to a birth accident, and who had been sheltered at home when her mother was alive.

Now, a new era had begun, and Fatima could stroll uncensored in the streets of Cupola Gardens, reaching the castle where the last king of Egypt, King Farouk, had lived prior to his exile. She bought coconut confections and biscuits at the market. At home, she clutched her portable radio, and listened to ballads. All this because Leila, the young mistress, had come back from America with notions of freedom, and let her forty-year-old aunt come and go as she pleased.

❈ ❈ ❈

"Om Reda, tell me a story," Leila invariably said after dinner, though she knew most of her maid's stories by heart. Om Reda felt pride that this learned woman, a journalist, loved her simple tales. She left Fatima to her radio, and sat on the floor as the mistress stretched on her bed. Om Reda recounted that she was *batted* as a newborn. "My mother spread bat's blood over my arms, legs, and privates so that I wouldn't have any body hair." Leila raised her eyebrows, and Om Reda uncovered her hairless arms and underarms, saying she never had to make "sweets," that sticky mixture of sugary water that jelled into a depilatory wax.

"Could bat's blood work for me?" Leila smiled.

"This needs to be done at birth, but I can make you sweets if you like," Om Reda said.

❉ ❉ ❉

A summer breeze rushed through the kitchen window. Om Reda sat on a stool, her black *jellaba* hitched up her legs as she minced jute leaves and garlic on a short wooden table.

"May your birthday be happier with the one you love. Lala Lala." Om Reda's full cheeks stretched as she hummed the song. "Lady, I have some news,"she said when Leila walked in the kitchen.

"Good tidings, *Inshallah*." Leila's upper lip perched on a cigarette. She opened a wooden cabinet with mesh grills and rummaged through the plates.

"Hosni *Bey*'s driver has asked for closeness."

"A thousand congratulations," Leila said.

"My intended is married. His wife lives in the village."

"You'll be his second wife?" Leila froze.

"It's better to live in grace than in sin." Om Reda smiled. "After the wedding, he'll give me money every month and we'll stay in his room by the garage when he's in town. His employer likes to visit the city a few days a week. My intended's name is Karim."

"A name that speaks of generosity." Leila's voice softened.

"My son is against him. I think he's jealous."

"Do you worry about that?"

"Well, Karim and I agree to wed. What can my little judge do about it?" Her laughter sounded brittle as she rubbed her discolored albows.

"Don't let your son stand in your way." Leila grabbed a plate and left the kitchen, black hair trailing in her wake.

❉ ❉ ❉

"Once in a place of wonder, to you of grace and distinction," Om Reda said, "there lived Hassan the brave. He was a humble man who fell in love with the beautiful Leila." Om Reda sat on the faded red carpet, the cracks in her heels stretched with her lotus posture, while Leila sank in her bed and fanned her manicured toes.

"Leila was a princess and her father would not consider her marriage to such a lowly man. The King asked Hassan to retrieve three emeralds hidden in the lands beyond the mountains. The King, in his wile, knew that no one had returned from this journey.

"Hassan bloodied his arms climbing cliffs. He battled invisible demons who yanked his hair and pulled his nails. He sifted twirls of mud at the bottomless lake, and finally found the three emeralds. When he returned with the prize, the king had no choice but to allow the marriage.

"Hassan the brave married Leila and people arrived from the farthest kingdoms to celebrate. The wedding lasted three days and nights. Hassan and Leila led a pure life and begat boys and girls."

Om Reda looked far away as she told her story and finished with her usual punchline: "What do you say? Was the story sweet or stale? If it's sweet, it is your turn to speak. If not, then tie me in a knot."

She lowered her voice as Leila fell asleep, with the light filtering through the long wooden shutters. Om Reda planned a nice garlic-coriander pesto to top off her *colocassia* stew as she walked back to the kitchen, her bare toes grasping the faded tiles.

❊　❊　❊

Om Reda had seen this family in better times. Fatima's father, the old master, was a Supreme Court judge who was chauffeured around in his Rolls Royce, and whose four-course meals were cooked by a chef and sous-chefs. Servants cleaned the house, personal aides ran errands, and a physical therapist came to administer bi-weekly massages. The judge's home library held books etched with gold. His wife was the daughter of the last prime minister of Egypt, before the revolution that promised bread and free education to the poor. The masses got bread and free education, but no jobs. The judge and his wife lost most of their vast agricultural lands to nationalization. *Politics were for the people of politics, and the rich*, Om Reda shrugged to herself.

On days when her intended, Karim, wasn't in town, she went back to her single-room apartment after work. Her son lived with her and banged the walls because he hated his laborer job and didn't earn enough to get married. She ignored his tantrums. Sometimes, she suffered a few bruises. In the evenings, she would light the flick of her kerosene burner, boil a cup of water, and sit on the porch steps, drinking tea and observing traffic, pedestrians, buses, and donkeys pulling carts. Sometimes she bought a few piasters' worth of salted peanuts from the peddler, or a roasted sweet potato. Life was always happening outside her door.

In the morning, she walked to work to save on bus fare. Leila would be at the newspaper's office downtown, and Om Reda cleaned and cooked, awaiting Fatima's arrival from her outings.

❆ ❆ ❆

Fatima opened the thin foil covering her biscuits and sipped her tea, stretching on the sofa. Purple veins traversed her legs like an exotic species of vine. Her smile revealed the perfectly aligned teeth of her dentures.

Om Reda sat on the floor, near Fatima, watching a movie. The television was enclosed in a dark wooden armoire. Leila Murad, that glamorous singer-actress with a heart-shaped face and a voice like a nightingale, played the role of a high school student who receives private language lessons at home. She sang light-hearted songs, teasing her taciturn teacher and mocking the rules of Arabic grammar, while serenaded by servants beating on tambourines. The lyrics urged the listener not to conjugate the past tense as one should let the past be and not worry about it. Fatima sang along with the classic songs she knew by heart.

Om Reda heard Leila's footsteps echoing in the hallway, as she headed back from the kitchen to her bedroom, a room the size of Om Reda's apartment, which opened onto a large balcony. The door was left ajar and Om Reda could see Leila's friend, Doctor Nina, sucking on her ebony cigarette holder and laughing with the robust mirth of her mixed French and Syrian ancestries.

A repetitive beat blared words that Om Reda couldn't understand, though she knew it was English. An herbal smell streamed out, reminding Om Reda of her son; she liked it when he smoked hashish because it made him less angry. He would lie back on his cot and smoke his hashish cigarettes till he burned his fingertips. *Tomorrow, I'll get a good job*, he would say. *None of that construction work*. But when he ran out of money, he always went back to the laborer's days.

              ❈ ❈ ❈

"Here's marriage reduced to its most elemental functions," Leila said, her voice reaching to the hallway. "I'm really confused by her choice."

"What other options would Om Reda have?" Nina said. "I mean, who else would marry her?"

"She's been a widow long enough, and she seems happy now." Leila said, her voice trailing.

"How old is she?"

"Old. In her fifties."

"Life is the art of the possible," Nina said.

Om Reda saw both women get up and dance, arms stretched to the side with jumping movements, like hopping. "I love Tina Turner," Leila said. The dancing seemed different from Arabic dancing, no swaying at the waist, no jiggling of breasts, just up-and-down movements of the arms, to-and-fro movements of the legs, and an occasional stomping of the feet to mark the rhythm. The women bent their necks, and tilted them back. American dance.

              ❈ ❈ ❈

"Pray on the Prophet," Om Reda offered her cue to the start of a story, a respectful nod to tradition. She sat on the floor by Leila's bed as late afternoon light filtered through the wooden shades. Dr. Nina had left to go back to her apartment.

"Upon him are prayers and salutations," Leila replied by rote, puffing on a cigarette.

"Hassan the brave received a visit by Hoopoe bird," Om Reda said, "and the bird announced: 'I have a beautiful bride for you. She's fair as the moon, her eyes glitter like the sea and her hair shines like a thousand grains of sand. But she has a curse upon her, which is guarded by an ogre in the land of Miraj. She can't move her legs, and she lies in bed all day, while her maid blots out her tears.'

"Hassan rode his horse into the night, and a billion stars whispered encouragement. He reached the land of Miraj. Pyramidal trees lined the road; they were bare except for black tufts at their extremities. At the end of the road, a sprawling castle flung its towers high in the sky.

"Hassan was stopped by an old woman at the gate. 'I can't walk to the river,' she said. 'Would you bring me some water, young man?'

"The path to the river was strewn with rocks and was far removed from the castle, but Hassan walked the long trail to fill her pail. 'Take this,' the old woman said, and her hand released a tiny seed. 'Don't ask questions. Just be on your way.' She kissed his brow and disappeared in a puff of air.

"Inside the castle, Hassan was startled by a creature sprouting tentacles. Serpents slithered on its appendages, and massive cockroaches covered its head. Tiny creatures with darting eyes crouched in niches along the walls.

"'Salaam,' Hassan said.

"The serpents hissed.

"'What brings you to the land of Miraj?' the ogre said.

"'I have a request.'

"'You have good manners,' the ogre said. 'Had not your salutation preceded your disputation, I would have smitten you right away.'

"'I heard you've hidden Leila's curse under your throne.'

" 'Afreet, Satan's minion, brought me the curse for safe-keeping. If you want it, you'll have to do something for me.'

"'What do you need?'

"'I yearn for a thing of beauty, but nothing ever grows here.'

"Hassan the brave brought forth the seed the old woman had given him, and placed it on the barren ground. He poured water from a pitcher, and lo and behold, the seed sprouted into a tree laden with fragrant buds.

"The ogre ordered his minions to hand Hassan the parchment that spelled out the curse. Hassan rushed back to Leila's castle and placed the curse in water. The ink dissolved, turning the water into a bubbling liquid. Leila drank it. She took tentative steps and started walking. The kingdom rejoiced.

"And so, Tutti Frutti, isn't this tale a beauty?" Om Reda said, and started to get up.

"It's a beauty," Leila said, "but what if the princess saves her own self, and marries Hassan?"

"This would be a different story," Om Reda said, squinting her eyes.

❊ ❊ ❊

"I left work early," Leila said, "and rushed to the police station to register for the referendum."

Om Reda placed plates and rounds of bread on the dining room table. The long table stood like an island on the floor tiles, an arabesque design of turquoise and black on white.

"Did you vote?"

Doctor Nina drew smoke through her long ebony filter, and expelled fantastic shapes, which dissipated in the afternoon light.

"This isn't a vote per se. This is just so we can say yes or not, whether we agree to have vice-president Hosni Mubarak as our future president. If the majority of voters say no, then they'll find another candidate."

"Who are *they*?" Nina said.

"I'm not sure. The parliament, the army."

"Why do you worry about such things? This referendum is rigged, of course. Our nations survive by *Baraka*, a mysterious grace," Nina laughed.

"Did you ever vote?"

"Back in Syria? Are you kidding?"

"I'm twenty-five years old and have never voted," Leila said. "You know what happened today? A police officer said it was too late to register, that I should have registered back in January. I've never registered since there was never an occasion to vote. Who could have predicted that Sadat would get killed? The officer said, 'What do you want to say, anyway? No?' and he spat on the floor, splashing my feet. I decided to leave Egypt," Leila said.

"You're so idealistic." Nina sighed.

"I'm going back to the States."

"What happened to your dreams of being a top journalist in Egypt?"

"I'm reporting on fashion shows. The other positions are political appointments. Journalists have to abide by a list of do's and don'ts. I'm suffocating," Leila said.

"Let's go to the Gloria Gaynor concert tonight at the Mena House," Nina said. "We'll enjoy the backdrop of the Pyramids, and kiss Egypt *au revoir*."

Leila raised her eyebrows.

" I've been accepted at the University of Paris, *chérie*, as a resident in medicine," Nina said. "The deal is that in return, I'll translate Arabic for the doctors. Lots of patients come from oil-rich nations to seek treatment in Paris."

"Congratulations. Looks like we'll both be out of here soon," Leila said.

"What about Fatima? She can't take care of herself." Nina said.

"I'll miss her, but my parents are retiring and will return from the States to stay with her."

"So you'll be all alone in America?"

"Yes." Leila's lips quivered as she looked away at the window. "And, Nina, how does it feel to be going back to the motherland?"

"Wherever I can get an education," Nina bit her nails. "I learned French from my mother. My writing isn't that good."

"Take some classes."

Om Reda sat on the floor, following their conversation. She rose to go to the kitchen and returned with a bowl of steaming okra. "Lady Leila, why don't you tell Doctor Nina the story of Hassan and the fate of doom, the fate of gloom and the seven seas?"

"Yes, we could both use it," Leila said.

Om Reda's tiny gold earrings caught the light as she sashayed back to the kitchen, smiling to herself.

❉ ❉ ❉

"The great sultan of Egypt dreamt that Hoopoe bird visited," Leila said, "and warned him that his life was cursed by three fates: the fate of doom, the fate of gloom and the fate of the seven seas. The bird scratched the sultan's face with his sharp beak and flew off. The sultan awoke and screamed when he saw blood trailing down his face. Soothsayers and necromancers rushed to the castle, consulting in his private chambers. They decreed that to avert these fates, the sultan needed a hero.

"Hassan the brave was summoned by the council and ordered to undo the curse. First, he had to find the cave of Babel. Hassan ran through valleys. He found a yellow ogre by a river, standing tall as a mountain. Hassan clambered up a date tree. 'In the name of the Almighty,' he said as he dug his spear into the monster's heart. Fairies appeared, sprinkled Hassan with gold dust, and guided him to the cave of Babel.

"Minions reached out from the walls, pulling his hair and *jellaba*. They spoke a language with clicks and snorts, and hissed black fumes. Hassan scraped his arms fending them off. When he was shoved against a latch, the wall split open.

"A thousand candles illuminated servants milling in red livery and a young woman reclining on a lounge-chair. Hassan was dazzled by her beauty; her blue hair flowed to her waist and barely covered her breasts. As he got closer, the woman changed into a blue monster with large boils and a single eye. The monster laughed.

"Hassan shot his spear into her eye. The monster shrank and disappeared. The cave filled with rainbows, and Hassan staggered outside.

"At the shore, he clambered up into a boat. Winds blew in fierce gusts, and large fishes snapped their jaws at him. When a fish flopped onto the boat, Hassan gutted it with a knife. Tucked in its entrails, he discovered a crumpled paper with a curse scribbled with illegible curlicues and rams' horns. He shredded the paper and scattered the pieces, saying: 'I banish this deed in the name of the Lord of Mercy.'

"The sea became as smooth as a lake. He rowed easily now, imbued with a superhuman force. When he reached the city of Ur, he ran to the king's castle.

"'Your majesty, I have battled the fate of doom, the fate of gloom, and sailed the seven seas. You are free from the curse of the evil one.'

"'Dear Hassan, you are brave indeed. I bestow upon you the lands beyond the mountain and decree you a prince.'

"Lavish celebrations took place, and Prince Hassan lived happily ever after with Leila, and they begat boys and girls.

"And so, Tutti Frutti, isn't this tale a beauty?" Leila said.

"I loved it," Nina said, puffing out waves of smoke. "There is no curse that can't be undone. A year of French lessons, and I'll be writing like Molière."

❀ ❀ ❀

Om Reda was getting married. She glanced up at the balcony, and smiled at Leila, Fatima, and Doctor Nina. Ululations and the metallic ring of cymbals rose in the night, a full moon gracing the sky. Fatima looked down at the narrow alley leading to the garage. She perched her arms on the sill, drinking her milky tea, a dreamy look on her face. Leila stood next to her and sucked on a cigarette. Nina sat on a chair, licking froth from her lips, a glass of beer at her side. She observed the proceedings through gaps in the ornate cement balustrade.

An old man sat on a rickety chair in the alley, his brown skin was etched by deep wrinkles, and he wore a conical red hat with a tassel. He sang of eternal love and happiness in quarter-note melodies, his knobbly fingers plucking his lute.

Om Reda wore a long blue dress and a scarf embroidered with red beads. She huddled at a distance from her groom, surrounded by her friends. Hurricane lamps glowed, and the groom wrung his hands as he balanced gingerly on a wooden chair. He had dyed his hair with black henna, a color that contrasted with his thinning pate. He smoked his nargila slowly, its water bubbles rising in a foamy mass, the smell of applewood drifting in the night air.

A handful of guests wore ill-fitting suits and gathered on plastic chairs set on the uneven tiles of the alley. They drank tea and helped themselves to heaps of koshary, topping the mixture of rice, macaroni, and lentils with fried onions and tomato sauce. Some grabbed chunks of roasted lamb from a platter.

Maids from neighboring apartments wore glittery scarves and crashed cymbals using their thumbs and middle fingers; the metallic sound rose with piercing clarity, like a trumpet call. The gray cat weaved between their legs, licking scraps off the floor. Palm trees swayed gently. An owl disappeared with a flutter, and constellations shone in a clear sky. The garage door at the end of the alley was open, revealing a black Oldsmobile in the light of the single bulb. The door to Karim's room, by the side of the garage, was festooned with colorful lights.

One of the maids circled Om Reda's head with a thurible and chanted: "I protect you from the evil eye five times, and another five times," as fumes flitted out of the incense burner's perforations.

Suddenly, Om Reda stood up. Her cheeks were tinted a florid red, and her lips were grossly rouged. A necklace of Indian jasmine hung from her neck, dangling on her ample bosom. She tied a scarf around her hips and her dress hitched up revealing a thick silver anklet. She walked toward her husband, bent down to kiss his cheeks, and shook her hips in his face. She ululated, and the maids responded with a crescendo of their own. It was a sound beyond words, beyond music: a guttural sound that hearkened to ancient times and seemed to pause the proceedings.

"A blessed night," said the musician, his conical hat tilting forward as he exerted himself on the lute, producing complex melodies with a harried beat.

One of the maids, a woman with a long, thin face, said, "The night of entry," and she blushed, and the other maids giggled.

Om Reda bobbed her head, stretched her arms, and moved her legs back and forth. She stomped her feet, and her ankle bracelet jingled. As the guests watched, she smiled and disco-danced to the ancient beats.

Christopher Woods, "Pilgrimage," photograph

Here Are Your Humans

entering from opposite edges
of the scene: a wood in spring (perhaps),
white splotches of dogwood blossoms
obscuring their features intermittently
as they move toward center stage.

You will want to know
they are a man and a woman.
(Surely you can fill in their ages,
their appearance — blonde-blue, tall-dark,
yes? — to match your preference.
Perhaps you wished for two men
or two women or two children.
One lonely romantic? All right, then.)

They approach each other,
eyes bright in the potential air
(the romantic and his loneliness, too),
the springy leaf litter releasing
a loamy aroma with each step.

Do they know each other
or are they strangers whose meeting
is fated along with the change
in weather and the shy trillium unfolding
whitely on the background hillside?
(Or is the season for trillium past?
Never mind, this is not the flowers' story.)

Now they are center stage,
and because it is spring
they will be lovers and exit together
into the next scene of their heartbreak
or happiness (represented by a dance).

And whose avid heart
doesn't follow after these, our humans,
who for us have made the trillium bloom out of season
and spun the stars on the ceiling
of our dark theater.

Presents, Please

In 2944, my birthday falls
On a Thursday. But that's getting ahead.
June could be gone. Thursdays. Self
Of course wants context to continue:
Super Bowl into clumsy numerals,
One war nudging another,
Modern moving evenly up
In *anni domini*, the cloth of calendars.

The party starts officially at 4:00
With Black Forest and ice cream —
Assuming flour and cows, cream.
An early bird arrival's fine.
We'll prepare the favors and funny hats,
Icing, a thousand candles on the sheet
Cake — assuming laughter and wax,
Matches, light! Imagine the light!

Eleanor Leonne Bennett, photograph

If Poetry Were Outlawed

Jimmy's at the blackboard shifting
his weight and fingering the crumpled paper
stuffed in his pocket that reads

with up so floating many bells down.
He's thinking about the buzz he'll get
when he reads it, nothing hard, just enough

to get him through the day. The girl in the back
is already gone, mumbling *I saw the best minds*
of my generation destroyed by madness and too baked

to hide the paraphernalia on her desk,
the scraps of worn paper, the old book whose pages
she rolls and unrolls between her fingers,

watching the words curl. In the streets a homeless man
begs for change but the pot-smoking professionals
pass him by and the corporate cokeheads too,

thinking, I know what he'll spend it on anyway,
and who can blame them? They've all seen him buying verse
on the corner, they've heard him ranting

April is the cruellest month. Besides, there's always someone
who takes more than he can handle, who thinks he's got
many and many a year ago

in a kingdom by the sea until the words start crashing
against his eyes and rocketing through his skull
and all he can hear is this mysterious

gravelly voice whispering *I celebrate myself, and sing myself*
and the world explodes in wheeling colors which rain down
around him and rupture into light. He starts running

into the streets where all the cars are shrieking around him
until they race him to the hospital where his girlfriend
runs up sobbing something about *hope*

is the thing with feathers and he starts begging for more,
his whole body in spasms, and he's shouting baby,
you gotta help me! And before they drag her

away she stands there soaked in sweat and tears screaming
THE APPARITION OF THESE FACES IN THE CROWD!
and oh

the sound just rushes through him, courses through his veins
until he shudders, gape-mouthed,
and lies still.

The Waking

He hacked through like the rest of them.
It was a lie, those brambles parted by God.
By the time he reached her he was sweaty
and thorn-scratched but she was too tired
to press her mouth shut once more and
feign sleep. It was all a lie—even the curse
had never existed, only a soft blessing
laying her down in the spinning room
filled with wool. She'd closed her eyes,
willed the court around her into a place
so like sleep that every ten years
the well bucket came up or the logs
burned down and no one ever noticed.
Those quiet years went on turning
beneath her pressed eyes—
until he burst through, dragging her back,
and suddenly there were ball gowns
and chickens and the stench of hay,
and everything bitter, bright, and hard.

Weaving for Odysseus

Blue is for you,
the creek of color which rises
from the boats of my shuttles.
Turquoise for your love,
for waves meeting a distant shore,
for your hand on my swelling stomach.
Gray is for the sky we share,
spanning the space between us
like a thread. Bronze is for your laugh,
for the glow of your smile
and the memory of your skin.

Black is for the first year.
For the second year, and the third.
For the horses who carried you away
and the distant soil beneath your feet.
For the eighth year, and the ninth,
and the son who has your eyes
and the eighteenth and the nineteenth
and the man who has my heart.

Red is for me.
Red is for my wasted blood.
Red is for the blistering of my fingers
as I pull out thread, tugging out your waves
and your soil, tearing at your horses
and your skin and your sky
and this year and the last
and the ten before —

as if I could rip out everything
but the pale skeleton of our love,
the empty loom of our life together,
and we the two sleek shuttles
rushing past each other
with a startled gasp.

Against Poems of Myth

For gods' sake, let Penelope rest.
Come here, just sit beside me on the ground
still packed and hard from winter.
Let's talk about the acid boiling in our gut
when we catch a lie. Let's remember
the wet crunch of cockroach beneath a sandal
on a night so hot we could feel the sweat trickling
down the backs of our legs. Let's talk about love
and arrogance, let's talk about stink,
let's taste the mouthful of bus exhaust
that makes us crave the city where we used to live
so many years ago, and haven't thought of since.

And if you start to float away
into the cupped dome of the heavens
where nymphs gambol and gods hand down judgments,
I will have to pin you down, grind your face into the soil
still packed and hard from winter, press my knee
into the wingspan of your back, show you that the blood
dripping from your nose isn't pomegranate red
and doesn't recall the sunset glow of Erytheia
but that it smells of railroad tracks and sweat
and turns the ground black and sticky as tar.

M. Shahid Alam was born in Dhaka and lived in Karachi and London, Ontario, before settling down in Massachusetts. Since 1988 he has been teaching economics at Northeastern University in Boston. His poems and translations of Ghalib have appeared or will appear in *Beloit Poetry Journal*, *Chicago Review*, *Quarterly Review Online*, *The Southern Review*, *Prairie Schooner*, and *Notre Dame Review*.

Mary Angelino has been published in *Best New Poets 2010*, *Hayden's Ferry Review*, *32 Poems*, and *Unsplendid*, among others. Her poem "Farmers' Market" was featured in the 2012 documentary *Up Among the Hills: The Story of Fayetteville*. Originally from Los Angeles, she lives in Fayetteville, Arkansas, and teaches English at the University of Arkansas, where she earned her M.F.A.

Damon Aukema lives in Red Wing, Minnesota, where he worked for many years with Lutheran Social Services. His translations of Scandinavian poetry have appeared in *Great River Review* and are forthcoming in *Canary*.

Wendy Barker has published five collections of poems, most recently *Nothing Between Us* (Del Sol Press, 2009), as well as three chapbooks. Her poetry has appeared in numerous journals and anthologies, including *The Best American Poetry 2013*. Recipient of N.E.A. and Rockefeller fellowships, she is Poet-in-Residence and the Pearl LeWinn Endowed Professor of Creative Writing at the University of Texas at San Antonio.

Eric Barnes is the author of the novel *Shimmer*, an IndieNext Pick from Unbridled Books, and has been a reporter, editor, and publisher in Connecticut, New York, and now Tennessee. He is now publisher of three newspapers covering business and politics in Memphis and Nashville. He has published more than 20 stories in a range of journals, including one that was selected for *Best American Mystery Stories 2011*.

Zeina Hashem Beck is a Lebanese poet educated at the American University of Beirut. She lives in Dubai with her husband and two daughters where she regularly performs her poetry. She's been nominated for a Pushcart and her work has been published in *Poetry Northwest*, *The Common*, *Mizna*, and *Mslexia*, among others. Her first book, *To Live in Autumn*, won the 2013 Backwaters Prize, judged by Lola Haskins, and is forthcoming in August 2014.

Daniel Becker practices and teaches internal medicine at the University of Virginia School of Medicine, where he also directs the Center for Biomedical Ethics and Humanities and edits Hospital Drive.

MICHAEL BOCCARDO's poems have appeared in various journals including *The Southern Review, Prairie Schooner, Kestrel, Border Crossing, The Pinch, Best New Poets 2013*, and others. A three-time Pushcart nominee, as well as a multiple recipient of the Dorothy Sargent Rosenberg Poetry Prize, he serves as assistant editor for *Cave Wall*. He resides in High Point, North Carolina, with his partner and three tuxedo cats.

DEBORAH BROWN's book of poems, *Walking the Dog's Shadow*, is the 2010 winner of the A. J. Poulin Jr. Award from BOA Editions, as well as the winner of the 2011 New Hampshire Literary Award for Outstanding Book of Poetry. Her poems have appeared in *Margie, Rattle, Stand, New England Review, Mississippi Review*, and other publications. She is a professor of English at the University of New Hampshire-Manchester.

LAUREN CAMP is the author of two volumes of poetry, most recently *The Dailiness*, selected by *World Literature Today* as an "Editor's Pick." Her poems have appeared in journals including *Brilliant Corners, Beloit Poetry Journal*, and *Linebreak*. She hosts "Audio Saucepan," a global music/poetry program on Santa Fe Public Radio, and writes the blog *Which Silk Shirt*.

WALTER CANNON is Professor of English at Central College in Pella, Iowa, where he teaches courses in early modern literature and writing. His poems have appeared in a variety of journals and reviews including *Flyway, Mid-American Review, Blue Earth Review, Water~Stone Review*, and *Nimrod*. His chapbook, *The Possible World* (Finishing Line Press) was published in 2013.

CHRISTINA COOK is the author of *Lake Effect* (Finishing Line Press, 2012). Her most recent work has appeared in *New Ohio Review, Crab Orchard Review, Hayden's Ferry Review*, and *Cimarron Review*. She is a contributing editor for *Cerise Press* and an assistant editor of *Inertia*, and works as the senior writer for the president of Dartmouth College.

CAITLIN COWAN's poetry has appeared in *Faultline, Mississippi Review, Poet Lore, Fugue*, and elsewhere. She has been the recipient of the *Mississippi Review* Prize, The Ron McFarland Prize for Poetry, and an Avery Hopwood Award. She holds an M.F.A. from The New School and will complete a Ph.D. at The University of North Texas, where she is a teaching fellow.

BARBARA CROOKER's poems have appeared in journals such as *The Hollins Critic, Beloit Poetry Journal, America*, and *Green Mountains Review*, and anthologies including *The Bedford Introduction to Literature* and *Good Poems, American Places*. Her newest book is *Gold* (Cascade Books, 2013), and her poetry has been read many times on *The Writer's Almanac*.

ANNE DAMROSCH's poems have appeared in *The Baltimore Review, Willard & Maple,* and *Down East.* Her chapbook, *Entering The Story,* was published in 2012 by Finishing Line Press. She is recently retired from her work as a maternal child health nurse and lives in Burlington, Vermont.

BIDEL DEHLAVI (1644-1721) was the prolific author of four narrative poems. He is remembered as the national poet of Afghanistan and Tajikistan, where his poetry is recited by people of all classes to this day.

DANIELLE CADENA DEULEN is the author of two books: a poetry collection, *Lovely Asunder,* which won the Miller Williams Arkansas Poetry Prize and the Utah Book Award; and a memoir, *The Riots,* which won the A.W.P. Prize in Creative Nonfiction and the G.L.C.A. New Writers Award. She teaches in the graduate creative writing program at the University of Cincinnati.

DENISE DUHAMEL's most recent book of poetry *Blowout* (University of Pittsburgh Press, 2013), was a finalist for the National Book Critics Circle Award. Her other books include *Ka-Ching!* (Pittsburgh, 2009), *Two and Two* (Pittsburgh, 2005), and *Queen for a Day: Selected and New Poems* (Pittsburgh, 2001). She teaches at Florida International University.

SCOTT ELDER lived as a busker and mime in Paris, London and Portugal before spending twelve years in retreat in a Buddhist hermitage in Auvergne. He now resides in France with his wife and young children. His poems have been published by *Plein Page* and *Poetry Cornwall* and will be forthcoming in *Orbis Quarterly International Journal, The Antigonish Review,* and *Poetry Salzburg.*

ERIC ELLINGSEN moved to Berlin two years ago to co-direct and teach in an art school experiment started by Olafur Eliasson and affiliated with the University of the Arts. He edits a new online writing and art platform called *Tick* and has a small space practice called *Species of Space.* His writing has appeared or will appear in *Shampoo, Spoon River Poetry Review, Beloit Poetry Journal, World Literature Today,* and elsewhere.

CATHRYN ESSINGER is the author of three volumes of poetry —*A Desk in the Elephant House, My Dog Does Not Read Plato,* and *What I Know About Innocence.* She is a member of The Greenville Poets and a retired professor of English. She is currently teaching poetry workshops at the Antioch Writers Workshop and at Wright State University.

CLARA CHANGXIN FANG was born in China and immigrated to the United States when she was nine years old. She holds an M.F.A. from the University of Utah and a B.A. from Smith College. Her poems have been published in *Poet Lore, Quiddity International Literary Journal, Terrain.org, Cold Mountain Review*, and *Verse Daily*, among others.

NINA FORSYTHE has an M.F.A. from Bennington. Her poems, translations, and reviews have appeared in *Nimrod, 5am, Chiron Review, Taproot, Puerto del Sol*, and the anthology *Knocking at the Door*, among others. She's a three-time winner of the *Backbone Mountain Review* Poetry Prize. She teaches E.S.L., hosts a monthly Coffee with a Writer, and conducts creative writing workshops.

CATHERINE FREELING worked in theatre and as a public school teacher before arriving at poetry. In 2012, she was a finalist for *Nimrod*'s Pablo Neruda Prize. She has been a finalist in the *Rattle, Hunger Mountain*, and *Bellevue Literary Review* contests as well. Her poems have also appeared or are forthcoming in *CALYX, New Ohio Review, Poet Lore*, and elsewhere.

REBECCA GOULD is a translator of Persian, Russian, and Georgian poetry. Her work has appeared in *The Hudson Review, Guernica*, and *Literary Imagination*. Her translated volume, *After Tomorrow the Days Disappear: Poems of Hasan Sijzi of Delhi*, is forthcoming from Northwestern University Press. She has received fellowships from the National Endowment for the Humanities and the American Association of Literary Translators.

JANICE GREENWOOD is working on her first book of poetry. She teaches creative writing at Mohawk College in Hamilton, Ontario. Her poems have recently appeared in *Arc Poetry Magazine, DIAGRAM, Cimarron Review, New England Review*, and elsewhere.

JEFF GUNDY's fourth prose book, *Songs from an Empty Cage* (Cascadia Publishing) is just out, as is *Somewhere Near Defiance*, his sixth book of poems (Anhinga). Other recent work is in *The Sun, Saint Katherine Review, Shenandoah, Rhubarb Magazine*, and *The Georgia Review*. He teaches at Bluffton University in Ohio.

LEO HABER's well-received novel, *The Red Heifer* (Syracuse University Press, 2001), was reissued in paperback in 2005. He has published a story and two poems in John Wiley & Sons' anthologies, *Best Jewish Writing (2002)* and *(2003)*. He is the longtime editor of the American-Jewish journal *Midstream*, after years of teaching Hebrew, English, and Latin at secondary and college levels.

JOHN HAGGERTY is an M.F.A. candidate at San Francisco State University. His short fiction has appeared in *Confrontation, The MacGuffin, Santa*

Monica Review, and *War, Literature and the Arts,* among other publications. He is currently finishing his novel, *Saline Springs,* which is a finalist for the 2013 James Jones First Novel Fellowship.

JARED HAREL's poems have appeared or are forthcoming in *Tin House, Ecotone, The Threepenny Review, The American Poetry Review,* and elsewhere. His poetry chapbook, *The Body Double,* was recently published by Brooklyn Arts Press. He lives in Astoria, New York, and plays drums for the New York City-based rock band, The Dust Engineers.

PAAL-HELGE HAUGEN is a much-acclaimed Norwegian poet and dramatist. He is the author of more than fifteen books of poetry, including a recent four-volume collection entitled *Kvartett 2008.* His work has been translated into more than twenty languages.

PATRICIA HAWLEY, a former creative writing/drama teacher, has enjoyed volunteering in local schools and serving on the board of The Skagit River Poetry Project/Festival in La Conner, Washington. Her publications include a first-place Prize from the 2011 25th Anniversary Tennessee Williams Poetry Contest, and an Honorable Mention in *Nimrod*'s 2011 Pablo Neruda Poetry Contest.

LINDA HILLRINGHOUSE holds an M.F.A. from Columbia University. She has received fellowships from the Macdowell Colony, Yaddo, and the Virginia Center for the Creative Arts. She has taught literature and writing to police in New York City and at Passaic County Community College in Paterson, New Jersey. In 2012, she was the second-place winner of *Nimrod*'s Pablo Neruda Prize for Poetry.

IRENE BLAIR HONEYCUTT has won awards for her poetry and teaching. Her most recent poetry manuscript, *Before the Light Changes* (Main Street Rag Publishing), was one of two finalists in the 2009 Brockman-Campbell Book Award Contest. Her work has been published by journals that include *Nimrod, Southern Poetry Review,* and *The Virginia Quarterly Review.* She lives in Indian Trail, North Caroline

PATTY HOUSTON teaches creative writing and composition at the University of Cincinnati. Recently, her work has appeared in *The Louisville Review, Oxford American, The Fiddlehead, Witness, The Greensboro Review,* and other journals. Her novel, *A Short Family History,* and her short story collection, *Wakigatame,* are in search of good homes.

NADIA IBRASHI's work received prizes with The National Federation of State Poetry Societies, Poetry Society of Michigan, and others, and appears in *Narrative Magazine, Quiddity International Literary Journal, The South East Review, Alimentum, The MacGuffin, Atticus Review,* and others. She is assistant editor at *Narrative Magazine,* and graduated from The Writers' Institute, CUNY. She has practiced medicine in Egypt and in the U.S.

ADRIANNE KALFOPOULOU is the author of two poetry collections, most recently *Passion Maps* (Red Hen Press). Her essays and poems have appeared in various journals including *Hotel Amerika, Essays & Fictions,* and *World Literature Today. Ruin,* a collection of lyric essays, is forthcoming in 2014. She teaches at Hellenic American University in Athens, Greece, and is on the adjunct faculty of the creative writing program at New York University.

HOLLY KARAPETKOVA's poetry, prose, and translations from the Bulgarian have appeared in *Mid-American Review, Huffington Post, 32 Poems,* and many other places. Her first book, *Words We Might One Day Say,* won the Washington Writers' Publishing House Prize for Poetry.

LIZ KAY is a founding editor of Spark Wheel Press and the journal *burntdistrict.* Her work has appeared in such journals as *Beloit Poetry Journal, Sugar House Review, RHINO Poetry,* and *Willow Springs.* Her chapbook, *Something to Help Me Sleep,* was published by {dancing girl press} in 2012.

JESSE LEE KERCHEVAL is the author of twelve books, including the poetry collection *Cinema Muto,* winner of the *Crab Orchard* Open Selection Award and *The Alice Stories,* winner of the *Prairie Schooner* Fiction Book Prize. She is the editor of *América invertida,* a bilingual anthology of younger Urguayan poets, forthcoming from The University of New Mexico Press.

ROBERT KING's first book, *Old Man Laughing,* was a finalist for the 2008 Colorado Book Award in Poetry, and his second, *Some of These Days,* appeared in 2013 from Conundrum Press. He recently won the Grayson Books Chapbook Competition with *Rodin & Co.* He lives in Greeley, Colorado, where he directs the website www.ColoradoPoetsCenter.org.

TAYLER KLEIN is completing her Master's degree in English with an emphasis in Creative Writing at Pittsburg State University in Pittsburg, Kansas. Her poems have previously appeared in *Analecta Literary and Arts Journal* and *Lalitamba* and she was a featured poet on Kansas poet Caryn Mirriam-Goldberg's blog. She resides in Kansas City.

CAROLYN KREITER-FORONDA served as Virginia's Poet Laureate from 2006 to 2008. She has published six poetry books and co-edited two anthologies. Her poems have received numerous awards and appear widely in journals, including *Nimrod, Prairie Schooner, Mid-American Review, Best of Literary Journals*, and *Poet Lore*. A painter and educator, she teaches art-inspired writing workshops for the Virginia Museum of Fine Arts.

MATTHEW LANDRUM's poems and translations have appeared in *Salamander, Beloit Poetry Journal*, and *Memoir Journal*. He lives in Ann Arbor, Michigan, where he teaches at a private high school for students with Asperger's syndrome.

MERCEDES LAWRY has published poetry in such journals as *Poetry, Prairie Schooner, RHINO Poetry, Nimrod, Poetry East, Saint Ann's Review*, and others. She has received awards from the Seattle Arts Commission, Hugo House, and Artist Trust. Her chapbook, *There are Crows in My Blood*, was published in 2007 and another chapbook, *Happy Darkness*, was released in 2011. She lives in Seattle.

CIRCE MAIA is the author of nine books of poetry. Her collected poems, *Circe Maia: Obra poética*, was published in Uruguay in 2011. In 2013, she was awarded the Delmira Agustini Medal of Art by Uruguayan President José Mujica.

DAWN McGUIRE is a neurologist and author of *The Aphasia Café*, winner of the 2013 Indie Book Award. Her poems appear in *The Ledge Poetry & Fiction Magazine, ZYZZYVA, JAMA, The Journal of the American Academy of Neurology*, and elsewhere. She received the Campbell Corner Prize for "poems that treat larger themes with lyric intensity" and received a 2013 *Narrative* best-of-the-year poetry award.

ASHLEY ANNA McHUGH's debut poetry collection, *Into These Knots*, was the 2010 winner of *The New Criterion* Poetry Prize. More recently, LATR Editions has released her chapbook, *Become All Flame*. She was the 2009 winner of the Morton Marr Poetry Prize, and her poems have appeared in *The New Criterion, DIAGRAM, Measure, Anti-*, and *The Hopkins Review*, among other journals.

PAUL MIHAS has taught creative writing at Duke University Continuing Studies and independently for over ten years. He is the recipient of the Thomas Wolfe Fiction Prize (2008) and the Katherine Anne Porter Prize for Fiction (2008). His short stories have been published in *Prairie Schooner, Talking River, Nimrod*, and *Best of the West: New Stories from the Wide Side of the Missouri*.

NANCY CAROL MOODY's work has appeared in *The Journal, Salamander, The New York Quarterly, Fjords*, and *The Los Angeles Review*. She is the author of *Photograph with Girls* (Traprock Books) and has just completed a new manuscript titled *Negative Space*. She lives in Eugene, Oregon.

MARY MOORE's work is forthcoming in *Unsplendid* and *Cider Press Review*, and has appeared in *Drunken Boat, Birmingham Poetry Review, Nimrod, The Sow's Ear Poetry Review, The Evolutionary Review, American Poetry Journal, Prairie Schooner, Poetry*, and more. Cleveland State University published a first collection, *The Book of Snow*. She teaches Renaissance literature emphasizing gender issues at Marshall University.

FABIO MORÁBITO, born in 1955 in Egypt of Italian parents, has lived in Mexico City for 35 years. His first book of poems, *Lotes baldíos* was awarded the Carlos Pellicer Prize and his second, *De lunes todo el año*, the Aguascalientes Prize. He has published short story collections, novels, and essays, and translations of the complete poems of Eugenio Montale.

CJ MUCHHALA's poems have appeared in numerous print and online publications, and most recently in the anthology *Echolocation*. She has collaborated on several poetry/art exhibits, including an installation at the 2013 Southeast Wisconsin Festival of Books. Her work has been nominated for the Best of the Net award and twice for the Pushcart Prize. She lives in Shorewood, Wisconsin.

ANGELA PATTEN's most recent publication is a prose memoir entitled *High Tea at a Low Table: Stories from an Irish Childhood* (Wind Ridge Books of Vermont, 2013). Her poetry collections, *Reliquaries (2007)* and *Still Listening* (1999), were both published by Salmon Poetry, Ireland. A native of Dublin, Ireland, she now lives in Burlington, Vermont, where she teaches poetry and creative writing at the University of Vermont.

GAIL PECK is the author of six books of poetry. Her poems and essays have appeared in *The Southern Review, Nimrod, The Greensboro Review, Brevity, Connotation Press, The Comstock Review, Stone Voices*, and elsewhere. Poems have been nominated for a Pushcart, and her essay, "Child Waiting," was selected as a "notable" for *Best American Essays 2013*.

DAVID A. PORTER was a co-founder and the managing editor of *20 Pounds of Headlights*, a literary annual, and he is the editor at large for *Caught in the Carousel*, a monthly online music magazine. He has published comic strips, fiction, and poetry in *Cadences, Confusion Review, Hotel Amerika, INK, Open Wide Magazine, Santa Clara Review, Sojourn Journal*, and *you are here*.

DOUG RAMSPECK is the author of five poetry collections. His most recent book, *Original Bodies*, was selected for the Michael Waters Poetry Prize and is forthcoming by *Southern Indiana Review* Press. His poems have appeared in journals that include *The Kenyon Review*, *The Southern Review*, *Slate*, *The Georgia Review*, and *AGNI*.

ELIZABETH REES's most recent chapbook, *Tilting Gravity*, won the Codhill Press contest in 2009. Her work has appeared in *Partisan Review*, *The Kenyon Review*, *AGNI*, *New England Review*, and *North American Review*, among other journals. She teaches poetry in the Washington, D.C., area.

JOHN J. RONAN is a National Endowment for the Arts Fellow in Poetry. His most recent book, *Marrowbone Lane*, appeared in 2009 (Backwaters Press), and was Highly Recommended by the Boston Authors Club. His poems have appeared in *Confrontation*, *Folio*, *The Threepenny Review*, *The Recorder*, *The Hollins Critic*, *New England Review*, *Southern Poetry Review*, *The Louisville Review*, *The Greensboro Review*, and *Notre Dame Review*.

TERESA ROY enjoys a higgledy-piggledy lifestyle in southwestern Indiana, where she writes and randomly submits poetry to diverse publications. Her work has been included in *Kayak Magazine* and *Exquisite Corpse: A Journal of Letters and Life*, as well as regionally respected journals *Open 24 Hours* and *The Round Table*.

MARY KAY RUMMEL is the Poet Laureate of Ventura County, California. Her seventh book of poetry, *The Lifeline Trembles*, is co-winner of the 2014 Blue Light Poetry Prize and is being published by Blue Light Press. She divides her time between Minneapolis and Ventura, where she teaches at California State University, Channel Islands.

JOAN ROBERTA RYAN is a professional writer with a lifelong passion for poetry. Her work has appeared or is forthcoming in *The Atlanta Review*, *Roanoke Review*, *Calyx*, *Concho River Review*, *Off the Coast*, *Prick of the Spindle*, *Taos Journal of Poetry and Art*, the anthology *Poems for Malala Yousafzai* (FutureCycle Press), and other venues.

MARGE SAISER's most recent book is a novel in poems, *Losing the Ring in the River* (University of New Mexico Press, 2013). Her poems are found at *The Writer's Almanac* and in *Prairie Schooner*, *FIELD*, *Rattle*, and *The Chattahoochee Review*.

JORGE SÁNCHEZ teaches English at Hebrew Theological College. His work has been published in *Poetry*, *Southern Review*, *Indiana Review*, *Crab Orchard Review*, and elsewhere.

BARBARA SAUNIER retired from Grand Rapids Community College in 2010 after teaching for 27 years. Recently her work was recognized in *Song of the Owashtanong: Grand Rapids Poetry in the 21st Century*, edited by David Cope. When she isn't writing, she strives to advance in dressage and dedicates herself to her fifteen acres, two horses, and one good dog.

LISA D. SCHMIDT's poetry has appeared in *The Bitter Oleander Press*, The *Comstock Review*, and *The Evansville Review*, among others. In 2011, she was a semi-finalist for the Pablo Neruda Prize and the River Styx International Poetry Contest, and a recipient of Special Merit recognition for the Muriel Craft Bailey Memorial Award.

STEPHANIE V. SEARS is a French-American anthropologist and freelance journalist, living both in the United States and in Europe. Her poetry has been published in *Coe Review*, *California Quarterly*, *Art Word Quarterly*, *The Amherst Review*, *Empirical Magazine*, and *Aoife's Kiss*.

PURVI SHAH is the winner of the inaugural SONY South Asian Excellence Award for Social Service, and is known for her leadership fighting violence against women. Her book, *Terrain Tracks*, garnered the Many Voices Project prize and was nominated for an Asian American Writers' Workshop Members' Choice Award.

MYRA SHAPIRO's latest book of poems is *12 Floors Above the Earth*. She is also the author of a memoir, *Four Sublets: Becoming a Poet in New York*. Her poems were included in *The Best American Poetry* 1999 and 2003. She serves on the board of directors of Poets House and teaches poetry workshops for The International Women's Writing Guild.

LESLIE SHIEL teaches at the Visual Arts Center of Richmond and at Virginia Commonwealth University. She has received an Individual Artist's Fellowship from the Virginia Commission for the Arts. Her poems have been published in *The Southern Review*, *Crab Orchard Review*, *The Sun*, *Poetry International*, and other journals.

JOHN OLIVER SIMON has published in many journals and is also a translator of contemporary Latin American poetry. He received an NEA fellowship for his work with Chilean surrealist Gonzalo Rojas. He is Artistic Director of Poetry Inside Out, a program of the Center for the Art of Translation. His book, *Grandpa's Syllables*, is forthcoming.

NOEL SLOBODA is the author of the poetry collection *Shell Games* (Sunnyoutside, 2008) as well as several chapbooks, most recently *Circle Straight Back* (Červená Barva Press, 2012). He has also published a book about Edith Wharton and Gertrude Stein. He teaches at Penn State, York, and serves as dramaturg for the Harrisburg Shakespeare Company.

KATHLEEN SNODGRASS's translations of Fabio Morábito's poems have appeared in *Poetry London, Boulevard Magenta,* and *World Literature Today.* She divides her time between New York and Mexico.

INGRID STEBLEA's poetry has appeared in *Rattle, The Seattle Review, POEM, Boxcar Poetry Review,* and numerous other literary journals. She lives in western Massachusetts with her husband and their two children.

CELISA STEELE lives in Carrboro, North Carolina, where she serves as the town's poet laureate. Her poetry has appeared in *Tar River Poetry, Anglican Theological Review, The Comstock Review, Inch, Broad River Review, The South Carolina Review,* and others. In 2011, Emrys Press published her first chapbook, *How Language Is Lost.*

MYRNA STONE's fourth and latest full-length book of poetry is entitled *In the Present Tense: Portraits of My Father.* In 2011, *The Casanova Chronicles* was named a Finalist for the Ohioana Book Award in Poetry. She has received two Ohio Arts Council Fellowships, and her poems have appeared in numerous journals, including *Poetry, Ploughshares,* and *Boulevard.*

JOHN SUROWIECKI, a former Pablo Neruda prize winner, is the author of four books of poetry, most recently *Flies,* a semi-epic poem about old age, death and insect life. He is currently working on a book of poems called *Foolishness.*

NANCY TAKACS is a recipient of a 2014 Ucross artist residency, the 2013 Sherwin W. Howard Poetry Prize for the best poems in *Weber—the Contemporary West,* the Nation Discovery Award, and the Kay Saunders New Poet Prize. She has three poetry chapbooks and one book published. A new book is forthcoming from Blue Begonia Press.

KELLY TERWILLIGER's poems have appeared in *Atlanta Review, Prairie Schooner, Hunger Mountain, Poet Lore,* and *The Comstock Review,* among other journals. Her chapbook, *A Glimpse of Oranges,* was published by Finishing Line Press, and she is in the midst of a new book-length collection. She works as an oral storyteller and writer-in-residence in public schools.

WYATT TOWNLEY is the Poet Laureate of Kansas. Her work has appeared in venues ranging from *Partisan Review* to *Newsweek.* She has published five books, three of poems: *The Breathing Field* (Little Brown), *Perfectly Normal* (The Smith), and *The Afterlives of Trees* (Woodley Press), a Kansas Notable Book and the winner of the Nelson Poetry Book Award.

AMY VANIOTIS grew up just outside of Portland, Maine, and now resides in Portland, Oregon. Her poems are published or forthcoming in *Poetry East*, *Solstice Literary Magazine*, and *Pearl*.

JULIE MARIE WADE is the author of several books of poetry and prose including, most recently, *Tremolo: An Essay* and *When I Was Straight: Poems*. She has received the Lambda Literary Award for Lesbian Memoir, an individual artist fellowship from the Kentucky Arts Council, and a grant from the Barbara Deming Memorial Fund. She teaches in the creative writing program at Florida International University in Miami.

MONICA WENDEL is the author of *No Apocalypse* (Georgetown Review Press, 2013) and the chapbooks *Call it a Window* (Midwest Writing Center, 2012) and *Pioneer* (Thrush Press, forthcoming Spring 2014). She holds an M.F.A. in Creative Writing from New York University and was the former writer-in-residence at the Jack Kerouac Project of Orlando, Florida. She lives in Brooklyn.

JOHN WILLIAMS is the author of *Controlled Hallucinations* (FutureCycle Press, 2013) and six poetry chapbooks. He serves as editor of *The Inflectionist Review* and co-director of the Walt Whitman 150 organization. His previous publishing credits include *Third Coast*, *Inkwell Journal*, *Cider Press Review*, *RHINO Poetry*, and various anthologies.

ABOUT THE ARTISTS

ELEANOR LEONNE BENNETT is an international award-winning photographer and artist from the United Kingdom. Her photography has been on the covers of books and magazines in the United States and Canada.

KIM BULTMAN is a writer, musician, and photographer from Eufaula, Oklahoma. When she's not playing the piano or wandering the shores of Lake Eufaula, she can be found in the kitchen, cooking up adventures for her blog, www.alittlelunch.com.

SHEILA CANTRELL has exhibited her work in solo and group exhibitions across the U.S. She is represented in Tulsa by M. A. Doran Gallery.

GLENN HERBERT DAVIS was the recipient of a Oklahoma Visual Arts Fellowship in 2006. His work has been exhibited and published nationally. His solo work, "image of one," was exhibited at Berry College.

KATHRYN DUNLEVIE'S work has been featured in *The New York Times*, the *San Francisco Chronicle*, the *San Jose Mercury News*, and *Artweek*, as well as internationally in *La Fotografia Actual*, *Art of England*, and *Profifoto*.

BOB EVANS has been making images for the pass four decades and has been published in various literary journals. He lives in northern Wyoming with his wife who raises dairy goats.

AMANDA GANNON is a self-taught author and artist from Oklahoma.

BROOKE GOLIGHTLY is a Tulsa photographer whose work has been exhibited at the Tulsa Artists' Coalition Gallery. Her pieces are often composed of several shots as she imagines "a world where wondrous creatures exist and people can soar as high as their dreams."

ELIZABETH SEEWALD HILL'S work has been exhibited across the U.S. She is represented in Tulsa by Joseph Gierek Fine Art.

SAMANTHA JONES graduated from The University of Tulsa with an English degree and a certificate in Creative Writing. In her free time she enjoys exploring creativity through photography, art, and words.

SAM JOYNER'S work has been selected for numerous exhibitions, receiving various awards. He is the Chair of the *Nimrod* Advisory Board.

SHOSHANA KERTESZ is a visual artist and poet from Hungary. She studied fine arts in Budapest. Her paintings and photography have been exhibited throughout the U.S., Hungary, and Israel.

ROI J. TAMKIN is an Atlanta-based photographer and writer. His photographs have appeared in *New Letters*, *Folio*, and *Nexus*. He contributes articles and photographs to *Skipping Stones Magazine*. He also exhibits his work locally through galleries and alternative spaces.

SHELDON TAPLEY has exhibited his work in solo and group exhibitions across the U.S. He is represented in Tulsa by M. A. Doran Gallery.

CHRISTOPHER WOODS is a writer, teacher, and photographer who lives in Houston and in Chappell Hill, Texas. His books include a novel, *The Dream Patch*, a prose collection, *Under a Riverbed Sky*, and a book of stage monologues for actors. His photographs have appeared in *Narrative Magazine*, *Glasgow Review*, and *Deep South*, among other publications.